NOW IS THE TIME

BOOKS BY FRED R. HARRIS

Now Is the Time
Alarms and Hopes

NOW IS THE TIME

★ ★ ★ ★ ★

A New
Populist Call to Action
by
U.S . Senator
Fred R. Harris

McGraw-Hill Book Company

New York   St. Louis   San Francisco   Düsseldorf

London   Mexico   Sydney   Toronto

Copyright © 1971 by Fred R. Harris.

Library of Congress Catalog Card Number: 70-150778

FIRST EDITION
07-026787-1

To my wife, LaDonna

★ CONTENTS ★

CONTENTS viii

★ PROLOGUE ★

"The future of this city? It's like a man with terminal cancer," a police sergeant in the Bronx, a borough of New York City, told me recently.

"I've moved as far out and as far away as I can and still drive to work," he added.

The policemen in the 41st Precinct in the Bronx, where not long ago I spent the better part of an evening just observing, call it "Fort Apache." That is how beleagured they feel.

The 41st Precinct had as many murders last year as the entire city of Boston. Pins in a map on the station-house wall showed locations where cabs had been robbed. One such robbery had occurred in almost every block in the precinct in 1970.

Walking around the country without a lot of press or fanfare, I had been trying to listen and to hear what people have to say. A young Irish policeman in the Bronx was one of many who had a great deal on his mind. Two of his sisters are nuns and he is going to night law school at St. John's University.

"The courts—that's the main trouble," he said, more with resignation than anger. Earlier an older policeman had put it more strongly: "I'd like to see some of those judges walk just two blocks out here some night, and they'd sing a different tune!"

The young patrolman was more understanding, but equally discouraged. "Most of the people we pick up are allowed to cop a plea [plead guilty to a lesser offense] and are back out on the streets again soon," he said.

"I understand it. I know there's no place to stack them in the jails until they could be tried. The courts and the prosecutor's office can't even handle the number that actually go to trial now. And I understand some of these judges not wanting to send people up to these prisons that are just criminal academies. They know most of those guys are going to come out better trained for crime than when they went in.

"I understand it, but that doesn't make it right. It's not the policeman's fault there is no money for better, faster courts and prosecution or to clean up these awful jails and prisons. It's not our fault, but we're still the ones that have to go out here on the streets and pick these guys up, knowing that it won't do much good and, before long, we'll have to face the same guys again, but next time they'll be a little tougher."

I walked the nighttime streets with Burton Roberts, the District Attorney in the Bronx, a real professional.

"What are you going to do?" he asks me, or almost anyone. "About ninety-five per cent plead guilty. It takes nine months or more to get the rest to trial. Right now, I've got 317 cases awaiting grand jury action and 1489 defendants indicted for felonies awaiting trial."

Twice during our walk in one area, anger at the wretched living conditions welled up so strongly in Roberts that he had to let it out. "Look how these kids grow up! Look at all this garbage! Why can't the city even pick up the garbage?"

"What chance do these kids have, growing up like this?" he demanded.

A young black policeman, dressed in civilian clothes —bell-bottom jeans—walked with us. He was supposed to work only days, but this was the third night in a row he had been out on the streets on his own time.

"Narcotics are our worst problem," he said. Passing a seedy café, he looked at his watch and said, "The junkies will be around here for connections in about thirty minutes." It was ten-thirty at night, and I asked if this would generally be the last for most addicts.

"No," he answered, "most of them will still need one more three-dollar bag or nickle bag to make the night." He was speaking of heroin. "Sometimes it depends on how strong a man's habit is or how much the stuff's been cut."

I asked if things were getting any better.

"No, it keeps on getting worse" was his response. "And education doesn't seem to do any good. Most of these kids on the street know more about drugs by the time they are twelve than we can teach them. They've watched people overdose. They know what it means to have to support a fifty-dollar-a-day or seventy-five-dollar-a-day habit. But still they do it. They go into it with their eyes wide open."

"What makes them do it?" I asked.

"They don't believe in anything any more," he said. "I don't mean just religion. They don't believe in religion any more, either. But they don't believe in anything else. Senators and Congressmen come down here —with all due respect, Senator—and nothing ever happens; things just get worse. They just think that things are hopeless," he added.

"Do you think that not believing in anything is also behind the growing drug problem in the suburbs?" I asked.

"There's that," he answered, "but there's more, too. There, there's also rebellion. Here, there's not so much of rebellion; it's just a hopelessness."

Not long after that, I was visiting with my father, a very small farmer in Southwestern Oklahoma, and his sister, my Aunt Audrey.

"Audrey said she heard you say on the radio that people like me are paying too much taxes, and a lot of rich people are not paying enough," my father said.

"That's right," I replied.

"Well, I told Audrey, 'Isn't he one of those who put them on us to start with?'" He meant it as a joke, but there was a point to be noted there. My Aunt Audrey made it clearer.

She talked of the fact that her husband had just suffered a stroke and that though he had worked all his life and she was working as hard as she could, running a small café for high school students in the little town where she lived and where I grew up, there was no way she could pay the medical bills. She knew this, too, along with tax reform, was a major concern of mine in the Senate.

The point is: Despite the confidence they have in me and as much as they like me, my father and my aunt strongly doubt that the political system is really going to do anything about their admittedly legitimate complaints.

Traveling around the country before the 1970 elections, I found over and over again that too many others of our people also really doubt whether much is going to be done about things that are terribly wrong. Many even doubt that much *can* be done.

Thus, waves of apathy have spread across this land. It is not just certain young people who feel alienated. Great masses of our people, everywhere and of every kind, do not feel it makes much difference which politician is elected.

In the months which followed my resignation as head of the Democratic Party in early 1970, I had more time than before to reflect on this.

A lot of people had thought that Washington *Post* columnist David Broder was right when he said that my acceptance of the Chairmanship of the Democratic National Committee in January 1969, at a time when the Party was broke, heavily in debt, weak and badly split, was like volunteering to crash-land on the *Titanic*. Several times during the year which followed I thought his words made a lot of sense, though most of the Party's icebergs are above water and in plain sight.

It did not take me long, either, to come to agree with former Republican Chairman Senator Hugh Scott of Pennsylvania, who once said that the Chairman of the Party not in the White House must be a "thousand-fingered Dutch boy who rushes about the political scene plugging up the holes in his Party's dikes."

I cannot say for certain that political parties are here to stay or that the two-party system will endure. But I have felt that one has an obligation to help improve his own party as long as it lasts and can serve as a useful instrument to advance the public good. I have felt that one has an obligation to see that whatever influence his party has is brought to bear to move the country in the right direction on the basic issues which confront it and to help generate the solutions so badly needed.

At the end of a year as Chairman, I felt that I had done my duty by serving during a difficult transitional period following the 1968 defeat. We had begun the greatest party reform in history; through the Democratic Policy Council, the Party had begun to speak out responsibly on issues; the Democratic National Committee had become a more professionalized, useful organization; and we had launched a vital effort for a much broader financial base, built upon a greater number of smaller contributors. Much, of course, remained to be done.

At the time of my resignation as Chairman, I said I felt the need to be free of the constraints which apply to the Chairman's job. "I do not feel the Nixon war policy will work or that it is getting us out of Vietnam fast enough," I continued. "I feel this Administration is equivocating on fundamental issues such as race, poverty, education, and health. I want to be free to speak out on these and other issues. Now, I will be again."

While the Chairmanship gives the holder's words wider circulation and a greater audience than they might otherwise have, it also tends to cause a questioning of motives by some: "Is he just saying that because his partisan role requires it, or is he really sincere about it?"

That and other compromising constraints of the Chairman's job were worth living with for a while in order to begin to move the Party in the directions I thought it ought to go. But, having charted and supervised that beginning movement, I wanted a looser, freer role. And I wanted more time to think.

A story making the rounds not long ago had a white liberal complaining that "civil rights was a lot more fun before the blacks got into it." For too long, too many played around the fringes of our mounting problems, feeling good about good intentions while the problems grew worse. A brotherhood dinner with blacks once a year, for example, did not change the fundamental defects in our system which condemned so many—black, white, and brown—to year-round hunger.

Neglect and half-hearted action on too many fronts have brought us to a time when too many people feel that hope is a useless crutch. The times are confusing. The old solutions are not working. The old alliances are being severely tested.

We can go either way. Men may gain and hold power by turning some of us against others. Or we can begin to see that there can be new strength in ourselves, that the hopes of most of us are the same.

It is not the "long-haired hippie kid" or the "pushy black" or the "hard hat" who has caused our problems. We—all of us together—have caused them. And we can solve them if we believe we can and if we will trust one another once more. In the great mass of people there is strength, if it is turned loose and set free—strength enough to do what needs to be done.

But the people's strength is fettered by outmoded party rules, aging political institutions, mismatched priorities, obscured goals, and worn-out programs.

In the struggle to free that strength, the people can regain hope.

CHAPTER I

THE NEW POPULISM

According to columnist Stewart Alsop, there are fashions from time to time in the themes on which political analysts choose to write. In the first half of 1970, it was fashionable to write that President Nixon was an extremely shrewd and adroit politician, that he was riding skillfully the volatile currents of unrest which beset the country, and that the Democrats had fallen into his well-placed traps by such actions as opposing the deployment of the Safeguard Anti-Ballistic Missile system, trying to override his veto of the Health, Education and Welfare, hospital construction, and similar appropriations, and fighting his appointment of Judge Clement F. Haynsworth and Judge G. Harrold Carswell for membership on the Supreme Court.

Several answers should be made to these assertions. First, it must be said that, if these were traps which snared the Democrats, they were not sprung because Democrats stepped into them accidentally or through ignorance. We did it on purpose; we meant to do it. I hope we will at least be given that. We felt these were fundamental issues of right and wrong on which fighting lines had to be drawn.

Second, it should be noted that some of the very people who have written most admiringly about what a good politician President Nixon is would be the first to admit that, deep down, Americans do not really like politicians. President Johnson's image as a shrewd handler of men and political processes suddenly became a liability, rather than an asset, when the impression spread among members of the general public that they were being manipulated. I asked one reporter friend whether he really agreed with President Nixon's televised veto of the HEW appropriation. "No, of course not; you and I know better, but I think it was terribly effective with most people," he replied. I told him that I was not so sure that in the long run the people might not prove to be as smart as he and I were. His statement reminded me of the campaign for governor one time of a very ambitious man in Oklahoma. Most people I asked said they were not impressed with the man but they thought he was going to go over well with the general public. That man eventually lost the election because those who told me that they, personally, would not vote for him were a part of the general public, and they helped to influence the rest.

As a matter of fact, President Nixon's standing as a politician was not nearly so high as the comments indicated; the polls actually showed him lower in public approval than any President in recent history at that time in his term. President Nixon seemed to be doing better than he really was—partly because he was not doing nearly so badly as many of the commentators had expected.

It was pointed out as further evidence of President Nixon's skill as a politician that he had pre-empted most of the issues of the Democrats, particularly the environmental issue.

I have been in politics since I was twenty-one years old, and the one thing I know is that I do not know how to gauge the permanence of political issues or the long-term effect of taking one political position as opposed to another. Thus I have always thought that a politician was better off to do what he thought right; then he would at least be able to defend his position with some logic and sincerity.

It seems to me that any attempt to gain momentary political advantage by playing upon the very real fears and frustrations—and even hatred—which so many people feel in America in regard to today's young people is a costly strategy indeed. As columnist David Broder has pointed out, "The future of the country depends quite literally on its educated young people, for it is impossible to imagine that we can govern this country, manage its economy or provide any of its essential services without their talents and skills."

It may well be true that the more visible and vocal college students today are a minority of a minority, as some have stated, but it is also true that they are a "Prophetic Minority," as author Jack Newfield's book title put it, and these brightest of our students will be written off or turned off or ignored to our country's great detriment. "For the demands of this new generation are not selfish or short-sighted," Broder has written. "Their aspirations for this country are generous and humane. Their talents alone can give America a chance of achieving its destiny. To 'govern against the grain' of their thought, as this government is now doing, is to short change us all." And, in the long run, that will be poor politics.

It will be poor politics, also, to seek to profit from black-white problems rather than try to solve them.

Race is the central fact of American politics today, because it is the deepest and most dangerous problem of American life. But this is nothing new. When I first ran for public office at the age of twenty-one, two years prior to the 1954 *Brown* v. *Board of Education* case, race was then the most serious political issue, and it still was, sixteen years later, when I served as a member of the National Advisory Commission on Civil Disorders (the Kerner Commission). Race will remain the toughest and most divisive issue facing America sixteen years from today (and this is my prin-

cipal point) unless we finally, now, face it squarely
and meet it. Deep down, Americans know that it is
not right to discriminate in education, housing, and
jobs, but, deep down, they also know we have been
guilty of it. And more and more people have come to
realize that racism has been unbearably costly in lives,
money, and peace of mind.

The response of the Nixon Administration to this
central problem and basic moral issue is to give
open aid and comfort to the last-ditchers by taking
their side and by equivocation. Just when the more
moderate public figures in the South, for example,
were beginning to feel politically secure enough on
this issue to be able to say that nothing more could be
done except to comply with the law ("We've run out
of courts," Governor Robert McNair said), the hard-
liners were encouraged by government policy to hope
that the clock might yet be stopped or turned back.
The Nixon Administration went into the Supreme
Court and asked for more time to integrate Southern
schools, the President sent up the names of Judge
Haynsworth and Judge Carswell for the Supreme
Court, and his policies caused men such as Leon
Panetta of HEW and a number of Justice Department
employees to quit with a blast at the slowdown in civil
rights enforcement. Senator Edward Brooke, a Republican of Massachusetts, said publicly that he was
"dismayed" by the President's handling of racial issues.

The anti-busing debate in the U.S. Senate in early
1970 focused on one of the most emotion-packed issues

in the nation, but the purposely confusing and contra-
dictory statements of the Nixon Administration at the
time caused cartoonist Herblock to show the President
hiding under his desk when strong leadership was
required. As the debate on the Senate floor showed,
the Nixon Administration was on both sides of this
explosive issue, with each of the opposing sides—both
Senator Hugh Scott and Senator John Tower—claim-
ing the President as a supporter. Busing is a collateral
issue, but the discussion of it presented a new chance
to move affirmatively against the basic problem, which
the Kerner Commission rightly pointed out is "two
societies, separate and unequal." The question facing
America was, and is: What other additional positive
steps will be taken to make the right to decent education, health, housing and to a decent job and decent
income real for all Americans?

President Nixon's equivocation will not work. Neither a Republican nor a Democratic President can out-
Wallace Wallace. George Wallace or someone like
him can always say it neater and plainer, and any
President who tries to compete on that level will destroy himself and his party by alienating too many of
his essential supporters.

As is generally, if not always, true on this kind of
heated issue, one is likely to anger both sides by trying
to straddle the fence. During the anti-busing debate in
the Senate, Senator Sam Ervin of North Carolina
called attention to inconsistencies between statements
by President Nixon and his Secretary of HEW, Robert

Finch, and stated that "it would appear that Mr. Finch is working one side of the street and the President the other side." Franklin D. Roosevelt was right when he once said, "The American people are quite competent to judge a political party that works both sides of the street."

If the race issue is not really a critical problem, one might with impunity ignore it or refuse to take a stand on it—or even treat it, as White House Adviser Daniel Patrick Moynihan incredibly suggested, with a little "benign neglect." If on the other hand, as I believe, it is a critical problem which requires continued and urgent attention, it will get worse under the policies followed to date by the present Administration and the people will have been deceived. Ultimately they will realize they have been defrauded by those who have not tried hard enough to avoid that result.

This is not the time to run away from black-white problems. It is time for leadership. I believe that, even in the South—or, perhaps, especially in the South —the people know that times have changed. They want positive, frank, and honest guidance to help them and the country over the last rough spots. They are tired of all the rancor and division. They will support public officials who will, with reason and goodwill, tell them the truth, show them their own and the national self-interest in tranquilizing this issue through action, and call upon their innate sense of justice.

Much is being made these days about how blue-collar workers, or union laborers, or "Middle America" or "the Silent Majority" will not support a public official or a political party that stands up for black people. Such an assessment fails to take full account of the fact that what is opposed most (sometimes unconsciously) by this group of Americans is having to pay a disproportionate share of the costs out of their own lives and income. Maldistribution of wealth and income in America, despite all our talk through the years, is still with us. Taxes, social welfare programs, and economic policy have made no real change in the rigid economic stratification which has been a durable characteristic of American life. As labor intellectual Gus Tyler wrote in *The New Leader,* "There are few statistics about the economy, curiously, that are more constant than the distribution of income among the nation's 'fifths.' From 1947 to 1967—during two decades of 'liberal' reform—the top fifth remained frozen between 40–43 per cent of the national income; the next lowest fifth between 23.1–23.8 per cent; the next lowest fifth between 17–18.1 per cent; the next lowest between 11.7–12.6 per cent; and the bottom fifth between 4.5–5 per cent. The pecking order seems almost ordained by Hell—or Heaven, depending on the plight or power of the pecker."

Those in the lower- and middle-income tax brackets have been close to "revolt" because they have rightly felt that they pay more than their fair share of taxes, while a great many wealthy people get special treatment. That is why tax reform and relief are so important. Though the 1969 Tax Reform Act did not go far enough—and I and others voted for additional reforms that would have increased revenue by $3.18 billion— it was, by and large, some movement toward engendering a greater feeling of confidence in the fairness of the tax system on the part of those in lower and middle brackets. The Social Security tax system remains largely unchanged from its historically regressive effect as a result of its flat rate and limit on the amount of salary taxed. In 1967, the average take-home pay of a production worker with three dependents was still only $90.89 per week. With no national income maintenance system and with inadequate minimum wage levels and coverage, there are today millions of people working full-time, as well as millions receiving Social Security, who are still below poverty levels.

If the government is going to help black or poor people generally to the detriment of nonblacks or the near-poor, or if nonblacks or the near-poor have to pay an unfair share of the costs, the unfavored groups quite predictably are going to react unfavorably. That has been the situation in America for too long.

But we should not be misled by any romantic notions, popular in some quarters today, that the salvation of the country and the impetus for progressive social change will come primarily from the upper-income and better-educated groups. While many are, and will continue to be, of vital importance to this cause, it is still true, as Gus Tyler, writing again in *The New Leader*, said—citing statistics and studies showing that more high- and middle-income voters, more business and professional men, and more of those with college degrees voted Republican than voted Democratic in the 1968 election: "Clearly, the notion that the affluent are liberal is pure illusion. To depict the well-to-do as favoring integrated housing, for instance, is to indulge in wishful fiction."

Though some of the best progressive voices in America are among the affluent and most educated, and their support and ideas, as well as the energy and idealism of young people, are irreplaceable components in the construction or reconstruction of a Democratic majority, there simply cannot be a mass movement without the masses. And for the Democrats, those masses necessarily include both lower- and middle-income whites and blacks and brown people and other minorities. Without them there is no way to count up a majority. And unless all these groups who make up the American majority continue to stand together and make common cause, they will have no way to satisfy their wants or protect their common interests against those who would exploit them.

I believe there is a populist coalition which can be rebuilt from these groups that constitute a natural and compatible majority, if the just complaints and needs of its constituent groups and members are properly recognized and answered.

At the height of black-white tensions in early 1970, I met with a number of my friends who are Oklahoma City labor union business agents and who took me to task somewhat for opposing anti-busing legislation

and for supporting the Philadelphia plan, which the
Nixon Administration had first supported and then
backed away from and which sought to apply greater
pressure for more building trades jobs to be opened
to blacks. One of them named a conservative Congressman who took the opposite position from mine on
these issues, and said, "You're in trouble, but, right
now, he could be elected to any office he wanted." I
told the group that if they let anything split labor and
black people apart, if that historic coalition were allowed to disintegrate and they did, indeed, elect men
of the type he had named, they would get exactly
what they deserved in regard to minimum wages, unemployment compensation, right-to-work laws, economic and tax policies which favored the affluent, and
on other matters they deemed of vital importance. At
the end of a frank and free discussion, most of those
present agreed that blacks and trade unionists had to
keep their heads, and work together, because they
needed each other now more than ever.

The Reverend Jesse Jackson summed it up not long
ago when, addressing a mostly white audience in Chicago, he said, "I don't blame the white trade unionist
for not wanting a black man to get his job; and I don't
blame the black man for trying to get that job; I just
want to see a policy that will let them both have jobs."

It is not always easy, I know, to talk straight to people, but I believe they are, by and large, tough enough
to take it and smart enough to accept it.

The commonality of interest in regard to basic

issues is particularly pointed up by the fact that unemployment, under President Nixon's policies, in 1970 went up to 6 per cent. There had been official statements that jobless lines would purposely have to be made longer if the economy was going to be brought under control. And no safety net of an expanded job program and a real minimum income was offered by the Administration to catch those who were forced to fall out of the economy. President Nixon in his "Workfare" program, for example, only proposed 75,000 additional job slots, when just a 1-per-cent increase in unemployment means that 800,000 additional people are out of work.

One Republican official, told in Tulsa, Oklahoma, that a local plant had laid off forty workers, was quoted as saying that if the economy was going to be gotten under control "there will just have to be some hungry mouths."

One person said to me, in justification of Administration economic policies, that rising unemployment in 1970 was still "only" 5½ per cent. I said that reminded me of something the late Senator Richard Russell had told me about Thomas P. Gore, the blind Oklahoma Senator with whom he had served almost before I was born. Senator Russell said that, as a fresh young Senator from Georgia, he had spoken up at a committee meeting called to consider providing certain benefits for widows and orphans of those killed in the Spanish-American war, saying, "I don't see how you can call it much of a war; there were only 385 people killed in

the whole affair." He said that stern old Senator Gore
turned as if to look at him with his sightless eyes and
said, "Son, for those 385 it was a helluva war!"

"Nixon has stolen the Democratic Party's environment issue," a friend said to me immediately following the President's 1970 State of the Union address. It
was good, of course, that the President had joined in
this vital fight, but—as it turned out—the President
was talking about spending no more federal money
each year than had already been approved. I do not
believe that issues can be pre-empted, as magic
powers are obtained in sorcery, by merely calling out
their names. Action, results, pre-empt issues. If we do
no more than he recommended in regard to air and
water pollution, my guess is that a little old lady in
Chicago will wake up one morning and notice that her
wash on the line still turns sooty, or that a mother in
Los Angeles will notice that her children's eyes and
noses are still irritated by smog, or that one evening a
man in New York City will notice that Hudson River
water is still undrinkable, or that a fisherman in New
Orleans will notice that the oyster beds have been
ruined by oil. At that point, these good people and
others may begin to complain that they did not get
what they thought they had been promised.

Today's problems are awesome, and cleverness will
not suffice. We still have an opportunity to save our
environment and ourselves. We still have a chance, for
instance, to show that men can live together on this
globe, or in this country, or even in one city, as fellow

members of the same human family. The greatness is in us; it must be called out by leaders who can help us see ourselves as we might be and can inspire America to get its priorities straight and do what needs to be done.

The populist movement of the late 1800s and early 1900s was a people's reaction against the greed and exploitation and the inordinate concentrations of power which were too much a part of the rise of industry in America. They organized against the exorbitant rates and discriminatory practices of the railroads, the cynical financial manipulations of the huge trusts and combines and the determined antilabor efforts of the "robber barons."

The people banded together to demand the right of initiative and referendum—the right to initiate laws themselves and to nullify by popular vote laws passed by state legislatures often dominated by the interests. They insisted upon the right to elect their own United States Senators.

One must not romanticize this historical populism; it was not all good. But the example of a people's movement in response to radically changed conditions which had tended to reduce the power and importance of the individual contains lessons with modern application.

Our society has radically changed since the end of World War II. The swift growth of our cities, the rapid increase in the numbers and mobility of our people, the sudden expansion of knowledge and tech-

nology, and the advent of instantaneous communication—all these have placed individuality under heavier
attack and in greater jeopardy than at any time in our
history. Man and society are at war with each other,
and there is desperate need for a negotiated peace.

This task calls for a kind of New Populism which I
think has begun to emerge, characterized by the best
spirit of the *old* populism that, as reported by Norman
Pollack, "had a peculiar notion of freedom: man was
free only when society encouraged the fullest possible
development of human potentiality."

This is the philosophy which can and must rebuild
the Democratic Party and lead the nation, a philosophy under which it is not first decided what groups are
to be members of the coalition and then how to appeal
to them, but, rather, goals and priorities are established in terms of people and then pursued with the
firm expectation that the people will support the party
or candidate which does so.

More than most, as the son of a Mississippi-born
Oklahoma dirt farmer and former sharecropper, I
know that some people must quit looking down their
noses at middle- and lower-income whites, in the
South and elsewhere. I know that government must
do better toward responding to the legitimate complaints of these Americans, as well as others. While
making clear that talk and repression will not cure this
land of the awful curse of crime and violence and the
increasing use of dangerous drugs and narcotics so
symptomatic of a society under great stress, we cannot

be unmoved by these frightening concerns which require action. We have to understand why there has been a tax revolt and why it is not yet over.

Most of all, if we will but listen, we will find that all over America people of the most disparate backgrounds—the young college student, the militant black, the suburban housewife—are saying the same thing: we want to live in a society which believes in something, which stands for something, in which there are some obvious values and ideals; and we are tired of having so little power in helping make decisions.

The Democratic Congress did a lot in 1969 and 1970. It reduced the President's military spending requests in 1969 and 1970. Over the President's veto it increased funding for the people-oriented programs of health, education, and jobs. It passed credit-rationing legislation which, if the President had used it, could have lowered the amount the ordinary person paid for interest and permitted greatly needed housing construction to start up again at a faster pace. It took important steps in regard to tax reduction and tax reform to aid the overburdened middle- and lower-income taxpayer. It provided increased Social Security benefits. It extended the Voting Rights Act without weakening it as the President sought. It adopted the National Commitments Resolution and the Church-Cooper amendment and repealed the Tonkin Gulf Resolution to tell the President that the people's representatives in Congress were not going to be bound to support any foreign obligations not approved by them in accordance with the Constitution. All these actions of the Congress in 1969 and 1970, as well as the statement by the Democratic Policy Council of the Democratic National Committee, on the issue which had so divided it previously, that the "loss of life, the diversion of resources from critical domestic needs, and the disunity of our country" caused by the Vietnam war must be ended by ending the war promptly, indicated the beginnings of a new populist commitment to reorder priorities in terms of people and their deepest needs. And the 1970 Democratic campaigns furthered this theme.

We have made a start, but a great deal remains to be done if we are to allow the people greater power over politics, party, government, and their own lives and if politics and government are to be ruled, as they should be, by the idealism which the most basic needs of the people require.

Some have asked me how a person with the views I hold could get elected to the U.S. Senate from a presumably conservative state such as Oklahoma. Others have wondered how both George McGovern and Karl Mundt could be elected to the Senate from South Dakota, or Wallace Bennett and Frank Moss from Utah, or Len Jordan and Frank Church from Idaho. I asked Senator McGovern about this one time. He replied, wisely, "There are a lot of ways to put together fifty-one per cent."

There *are*, indeed, a lot of ways to put together 51 per cent. Nationally, rather than try to forge a negative majority around people's baser fears and frustrations, we must unite a positive majority around the people's better hopes and dreams. That may be harder to do, but it is worth the effort.

CHAPTER II

THE MAKING
OF A MAJORITY

"The Nixon Administration seems destined by precedent to be the beginning of a Republican era," wrote Kevin Phillips in 1969 in his book *The Emerging Republican Majority.* The old Democratic majority coalition has broken up for good, he solemnly announced. "The king is dead; long live the king!" And quite a few interested observers—both the delighted and the downcast—took his words seriously.

Some Americans may still worry about pollution, or education, or housing, or crime in the cities—for, after all, we have rapidly become a nation where 70 per cent of our people live on less than 3 per cent of the land.

But Mr. Phillips did not look at it that way. His charts and graphs and purported trends, instead, caused him to draw purely political conclusions: "The GOP is particularly lucky," he wrote, "not to be weighted down with commitments to the political blocs, power brokers and poverty concessionnaires of the decaying central cities of the North, now that national growth is shifting to suburbia, the South and the West."

It seems to be a variation on Horace Greeley's theme: "Go where the votes are, young man."

It was that kind of wrinkled-browed, tight-mouthed soberness with which Mr. Phillips analyzed and recommended with such self-assurance that gave new hope to a good many Republican professionals and caused more than a few battle-tough Democratic warriors to look apprehensively over their shoulders.

Who do the Democrats have left on their side? Phillips claimed they are the "establishment" and "silk stocking" suburban types who make their living as "research directors, associate professors, social workers, educational consultants, urbanologists, development planners, journalists, brotherhood executives, foundation staffers, communications specialists, culture venders, pornography merchants, poverty theorists and so forth." The Democratic team includes, he said, some poor people and some young people, too. But the main group the Democrats still have left is the one that ruined it all for them, according to Phillips: the blacks. "The principal force which broke up the Democratic (New Deal) coalition is the Negro socio-economic revolution. . . ."

If the GOP is lucky not to be politically obligated to worry about the cities, then Phillips must feel that the growing political activity of black people is for the Republicans, as we used to say in Oklahoma, like finding a bird nest on the ground, for he wrote: "Substantial Negro support is not necessary to national Republican victory in light of the 1968 election returns. Obviously, the GOP can build a winning coalition without Negro votes."

Not only can, but it is easier that way. "Indeed," Mr. Phillips declared, "Negro-Democratic mutual identification was a major source of Democratic losses . . . and Republican or American Independent Party profit . . . in many sections of the nation. . . ."

Put them all together, and, while they may not spell "mother," they do spell the next best thing for Republicans, Phillips believes, and that is "victory."

"One of the greatest political myths of the decade— a product of liberal self-interest—is," Mr. Phillips wrote, "that the Republican Party cannot attain national dominance without mobilizing 'liberal' support in the big cities, appealing to 'liberal' youth, empathizing with 'liberal' urbanization, gaining substanial Negro support and courting the affluent young professional classes of suburbia."

If there is a growing "military-industrial complex," as the late President Dwight Eisenhower feared, Phillips views it as a plus, not a minus. "For one thing," he wrote, "Sun country in general and California in particular house a vast complex of military bases and defense plants" which "logically tend to support patriotism, pentagon and paycheck."

This, then, is the Phillips thesis: There exists a majority conservative coalition, ready to be glued together permanently, consisting of the 57 per cent of the total 1968 vote which President Nixon and Governor Wallace, combined, received; write off the industrial Northeast and concentrate on the people whom it is now fashionable to call "the unpoor, the unblack and the unyoung" in the South and the suburbs.

In other words, as M. Stanton Evans, who ecstatically called it "the most important political book in this generation," stated in the rigid-right *National Review* magazine, the Phillips conclusion is an affirmation "that last year's Nixon victory completed the work Goldwater had begun."

Kevin Phillips is an intense young Harvard Law School graduate, who, during the 1968 campaign, inked in his map sections and lined out his charts while sitting at the right hand of John Mitchell, the chief architect and head guru of the Nixon candidacy. During the first year of the Nixon Administration he served as special assistant to Attorney General Mitchell, a post from which he eventually graduated to become a nationally syndicated columnist and pollster.

Soon after being published by Arlington House and selected by the Conservative Book Club, *The Emerg-*

ing Republican Majority, which Mr. Phillips had dedicated to its "two principal architects . . . President
Richard M. Nixon and Attorney General John N.
Mitchell," began to get a great deal of public attention. Liberal and moderate Republican Senators such
as Jacob Javits of New York, Marlow Cook of Kentucky, and Charles McC. Mathias of Maryland soon
thereafter began saying some unkind words about the
Phillips book.

Because of their expressions of alarm, GOP Chairman Rogers Morton came forward to disclaim the
book as the work of a "clerk" whose ideas could not
change the political profile of the country. But many
continued to worry about it because Administration
actions seemed to be in line with the book and because the same Republican Chairman Morton, for
example, defended the Nixon slowdown on desegregation of schools fifteen years following *Brown* v.
Board of Education, saying "Implementation of civil
rights laws has to be carried out at a rate equal to the
public digestion process. Obviously, that rate is different in Vicksburg, Mississippi, than it is in Portland,
Maine."

Attorney General John Mitchell was said to have
denied that such a strategy existed. But Mr. Mitchell
is the person who recommended Judge Clement F.
Haynsworth and Judge G. Harrold Carswell for the
Supreme Court, who asked the Congress to water
down the Voting Rights Act, and who asked the Supreme Court to approve a desegregation slowdown. It

was Attorney General Mitchell who also said "Judge us by what we do, not by what we say."

Unlike Senator Strom Thurmond of South Carolina, who wrote, "As the weeks go by, no one who has a concern about the future of American politics will admit to not having read this book," President Nixon, when asked about it at a press conference, passed it off with a chuckle and said, "I regret to say—and I hope this does not discourage sales of the book, which I understand are quite good—but I have not read the book."

In the same press conference, President Nixon said he was for the middle ground between "instant integration" and "desegregation forever," and later both conjured up and summoned out the "Silent Majority" to stifle dissent and display national unity on the Vietnam war, getting this issue down to the brass tacks of being for or against your country.

Vice-President Agnew, too, tried to cool off attention to the theory. But he also bareknuckled it with the kids, the "effete corps of intellectual snobs," "the ideological eunuchs," the "radical libs," and the biased Eastern television and press, choosing to speak some of those words loudest, by chance, in George Wallace's home country of Montgomery, Alabama.

"Under the circumstances," as *Fortune* magazine stated, "it seems permissible to question whether the Administration's leaders truthfully reject his theory, or merely are chagrined that he has spelled it out with such candid cynicism. It may be that Phillips has done for Ni on the same dubious service that Machiavelli performed for Cesare Borgia—describing in naked words what his hero had all along been doing by instinct."

"I like it, but is it art?" some Republicans ask anxiously. Just as anxiously, some Democrats whisper that they do *not* like it, but are afraid it is—that it will work, that it is working.

There are really two questions, a fact that some usually discerning reviewers missed. "Will it work?" is the obvious question most often discussed. "Should it work?" is the other.

Will it work? Aside from the fact that the strategy makes pariahs of a lot of people, such as (in Phillips' terms) "associate professors" and "urbanologists" and "journalists" and "communications specialists," who, experience shows, can have considerable impact on the opinions of others over the long pull; aside from the fact that such a distinctly conservative plan proved a disaster for Goldwater; aside from the fact, as recently pointed out by Professor Andrew Hacker, a Republican and a professor at Cornell, in *Commentary* magazine, that the Republican burghers and bankers who he says dominate that party's politics would have to change a great deal before they would truly welcome meeting-room shoulder-rubbing with the blue-collar men whose votes they crave; and aside from the fact that George Wallace, himself, shows every sign of again being a candidate for President in 1972 ("Nixon is doing what I advocated, and he said I was unfit to be President"), which could really

tear up the Phillips playhouse, there are other fundamental and structural defects in the Phillips grand
design.

For one thing, it is not so easy to characterize the
South and "Sun Belt" as so uniformly "conservative"
as they might once have been or as Mr. Phillips thinks
them now. Professor Polsby has shown that "Over the
last decade, for example, most of the liberal Democratic Congressmen from Texas have represented the
growing cities of Houston, Galveston, Fort Worth,
Austin, Beaumont and San Antonio," and that in the
South and Southwest "Republicans have replaced conservative Democrats more often than they have replaced liberals. . . ."

In a recent article, "The Liberal Republican De-
lusion," in *The New Leader*, Democratic New York
Congressman Bertram L. Podell made the point that
"A cursory look at new Southern faces" in the U.S.
House of Representatives shows that "almost all of the
Democrats are at least moderates, like David Pryor
(Arkansas) and Nick Galifianakis (North Carolina)."
And the progressive Republican Ripon Society calls
attention to the fact that "many of the GOP's top
Southern officeholders—including Governor Win-
throp Rockefeller of Arkansas, Senator Howard Baker
of Tennessee, Congressman George Bush of Houston,
and Mayor George Seibels of Birmingham, Alabama
— . . . won by appealing to just those groups that the
Southern strategy rejects."

The South is changing. Regular Democratic State

Chairman of Alabama, Robert S. Vance, who has launched new efforts to broaden the base of his party and bring in more blacks, recently made this point in a speech in Huntsville, saying: "The conflicts and conditions which made reconciliation of Democrats impossible a few years ago are rapidly changing. Old problems within this region are not being resolved overnight, but democratic progress is being made. New leadership is arising—new coalitions are being formed—new attitudes are taking shape."

Most results of the 1970 elections helped to bear out this remarkably accurate judgment and to undercut dramatically the Phillips thesis. In the spring, Atlanta chose a Jewish liberal Democrat, Sam Massell, as Mayor and elected a black liberal Democrat, Maynard Jackson, as Vice-Mayor. The infamous Carswell lost the Republican Senate nomination in Florida. Moderate or liberal Democrats were elected to governorships throughout Phillips' hunting grounds—Mandel in Maryland, West in South Carolina, Carter in Georgia, Bumpers in Arkansas, Hall in Oklahoma, and Gilligan in Ohio, for example.

Further, an openly conservative or anything akin to a racist appeal is already proving troublesome and will soon prove very costly for the Republican Party as a plan of action. As Phillips advocated, for example, it writes off the entire state of Pennsylvania altogether, despite the fact that it has had a liberal-to-moderate Republican governor (Raymond Shafer), and two liberal Republican Senators, one of whom (Richard

Schweiker) was just elected to the Senate in 1968, and the other (Hugh Scott), the Senate Republican leader, was returned in 1970—all of whom, rather understandably, have tried to dissociate themselves from the movement of the Republican Party more to the right.

Such an appeal ignores the fact that most of the Republican Senators who have come to the Senate since I have been there (Brooke, Percy, Schweiker, Saxbe, Weicker, Cook, and Mathias, for example), as well as a substantial number of more senior Republican Senators (Javits, Cooper, and Case, for example), and, indeed, Senate Republican Leader Scott and Assistant Leader Robert Griffin of Michigan will increasingly find it impossible to survive politically under the label of a Republican Party which is all-out conservative. When the Republican Party was not in control of the White House, it was easier for its candidate for President to fuzz up his position without angering either Strom Thurmond or Jack Javits on the issue of race, of example, or either John Tower or John Sherman Cooper on the issue of ABM. It is much more difficult now.

Republican attempts at a national conservative coalition under their banner is, as clearly indicated by the angry anguished outcries already heard from liberal and moderate Republicans in the Senate, causing severe stresses on Party unity which will lead to major fissures.

Apparently trying to salvage whatever political advantage he could from the Senate's rejection of the nomination of Judge G. Harrold Carswell to be an Associate Justice of the Supreme Court, President Nixon wrongly charged that the Senate was prejudiced against Judge Carswell because he was a Southerner. This irresponsible accusation not only served further to exacerbate painful regional divisions in the country but also caused considerable anguish among those in his own party in the Senate who had voted their consciences against confirmation.

Some of the more moderate or progressive Republican members of the Senate began, thereafter, to feel more and more cut off from the President. Several of them looked forward anxiously to the election in Alabama, which would decide whether former Governor George Wallace would serve again in that capacity and remain a viable national figure. "My only hope is that, if Wallace is beaten, the President will stop being so uptight about the threat to him from the right and begin to moderate somewhat," one such Republican Senator told me privately.

But that was not to be; with a blatantly racist campaign, Mr. Wallace was re-elected. And Kevin Phillips, in the first written product of his new columnist status, continued to play his familiar theme with little, if any, variation. "After studying the Alabama returns, the White House has decided against a shift in basic Administration policy," he reported approvingly. "Despite press reports to the contrary, the South remains a top Nixon target."

Continuation by the President down the openly rightward path, speeded along by repeated actions such as the dismissal of Commissioner of Education James Allen, produced increasingly open breaks with the Administration by leading progressive Republicans, such as Senator Mark Hatfield of Oregon, who said, "For me, this spells possible disaster for the Republican Party beyond 1972. . . . The rightward movement, the Southern Strategy, tends to create a more exclusive party and that, to me, spells an end to the Republican Party."

Though it is not my role to advise the opposition, I would just point out that the progressive wing of their party, while not yet dominant, is growing and is already too large to be ignored, except at serious peril to the future of the Republican Party itself.

Thus, another serious flaw in the Phillips strategy. He calmly wrote that "perhaps several million Republicans and Independents from Maine and Oregon to Fifth Avenue" under his recommendations would be lost to the Republican Presidential candidate. The Ripon Society has calculated that this planned loss (which sounds a lot to me like the late *Saturday Evening Post* purposely lopping off millions of its subscribers—and look how that strategy worked for them) would reduce Nixon's 43 per cent of the vote in 1968 to 40 per cent, and this, coupled with what Phillips would then hope to pick up from the Wallace vote, would, they say, only amount to a "cliff-hanging fifty and a half per cent majority—hardly the stuff of which political dynasties are made."

Phillips and other like-minded Republicans are more than a little incautious in basing so much of their long-range plans and projections on one case in point, the 1968 elections. If one feels that 1968 was a typical example from which to choose to generalize for all time about the direction politics is heading in America, he must also feel that the awful divisiveness of the Vietnam war and the urban black riots and student disorders, as well as the "throw the rascals out" baggage Vice-President Humphrey carried in 1968, will all continue to be with us for the foreseeable future, but will somehow next time work to the advantage of the incumbent, the man who will have been in charge for the preceding four years.

Or, do Mr. Phillips and others who agree with him feel that these (and, for that matter, the disgrace in Chicago) were not major factors in Mr. Nixon's election? And have they reflected that even with these factors it was an election which brought Mr. Nixon into office as a minority President with the smallest percentage of the popular vote since Woodrow Wilson's in 1912 and saw him inaugurated President at the same time both houses of Congress were being organized by the opposition party, something that had not happened since Zachary Taylor's election in 1848?

Or that even his slender plurality was slipping and Mr. Humphrey's vote was rising as the campaign ended?

Can one really, then, take President Nixon's 34 per cent and Governor Wallace's 14 per cent of the vote in 1968 and total them up to a Republican majority, as Phillips and others hope?

Not if there is real regard for the facts. Especially not, if one is realistic about Mr. Wallace's 14 per cent.

Mr. Phillips more or less sees the Wallace voter as a Democratic page, risen temporarily to become an Independent squire, but now ready to kneel down for the Nixonizing conservative touch on the shoulder which will confer permanent Republican knighthood.

Professor Hacker put it nicely when he wondered "what kind of an appeal one makes to citizens who once succumbed to the charms of an Alabama governor." He answered his own question partly when he noted: "In fact, most of the Wallace voters Phillips wishes to attract have enjoyed federal subsidies and services for most of their lives." And Professor Polsby has persuasively argued that party tradition, which he finds still rather strong and favorable to the Democrats nationally, and "pocketbook issues" will work against the Phillips thesis.

The fact is that Governor Wallace made strong endorsements of labor unions and the right of collective bargaining, demanded massive increases in Social Security benefits, and advocated important and meaningful tax reform—and these were by no means all of the nonconservative positions he took in the 1968 Presidential campaign.

In my own state, a national pollster in 1969 found that the persons interviewed were able to be quite accurate in listing all major political figures in either liberal, conservative, or moderate columns, but were confused about how to list Mr. Wallace; one-third thought he was conservative, one-third thought he was liberal, and one-third was unable to say.

In the same poll, a majority of those Democrats who said they had supported Senator Eugene McCarthy prior to the 1968 Democratic convention stated that they had thereafter voted for Mr. Wallace in the general election. Similarly, a Michigan State University survey has indicated that a large number of those who voted for Senator McCarthy in the New Hampshire primary either were not aware of or did not agree with his Vietnam position, and a national magazine found that steelworkers in Gary, Indiana, who had supported the late Senator Robert Kennedy in the primary there, after his death were leaning toward Mr. Wallace.

What does all this mean? It means that a substantial number of those who voted for Mr. Wallace in 1968 did so at least as much because of some of his populist positions as for racist reasons.

It also means that in 1968 there was a large body of feeling in America against the way things were and the people who were running things—and that at least some part of the appeal of Senator McCarthy, the late Senator Kennedy, and Mr. Wallace resulted from the belief that these three intended to change the *status quo* and that they were fighting against those who were in power. A conservative party and an incumbent President would do well, then, to delay enumerating the poultry prior to the hatching process, or however we used to say it in Oklahoma.

Indeed, looking for coalition, one might more easily and with more reason add up enough voters to make a majority by totaling Vice-President Humphrey's 42 per cent of the 1968 vote with the populist portion of Mr. Wallace's 1968 percentage.

As the Ripon Society put it: "Phillips recognizes Wallace's success in 'blending populism and some legitimate complaints about American society with an unspoken opposition to further government aid for Negroes' but having made this recognition, he proceeds to ignore it."

There are those who say that to counter the more conservative Republican appeal, the Democrats too must slick down their hair and make a courting call on the rightists. I do not agree, and that brings us to the second question concerning the new Republican strategy: *Should* it work?

I remember, late in the 1968 Presidential campaign, in Portland, Oregon, George Ball and I were sitting with Vice-President Humphrey in his suite, discussing the Vietnam speech he was to make three days later in Salt Lake City. We had just returned from a rally at which a small group had, as had so often been true throughout the campaign up to that time, skillfully

heckled the Vice-President, ruining the impact and
news reports of an otherwise successful meeting.
Mr. Humphrey was badly depressed, and he said, out
loud for the first time, that he doubted he could be
elected.

Up to that time, the Vice-President had been receiving two different kinds of campaign advice. The
sides had been drawn up early, and each side was
made up of equally impassioned and equally persuasive advocates.

One group of the Vice-President's campaign inti-
mates regularly stirred and studied the opinion polls
and brought forth the revealed truth like soothsayers
reading chicken entrails. They frequently alluded to
what they called the "non-marching majority," whose
average member was supposed to have 2.2 children,
1.3 cars, two-thirds of a boat, a mortgaged thirteen-
thousand-dollar house on which the payments were
seventy-three dollars per month and a television set,
one half of which was colored—or some such statistics.
They could rattle off the average man's views on every
subject with equal assurance, so the proper campaign
plan was obvious to them: "Nixon and Wallace know
their man; hit him with the old 'law and order' hawk-
ish axe handle," whatever the Vice-President's personal views.

There were others who strongly disagreed. I was
one of these. So was Mr. Humphrey, but that did not
stop them from continuing to work him over.

Sitting there in Portland late that night, after everyone else had gone to bed, we talked about these things.

He had made an extremely courageous civil liberties speech at a California state labor convention two days before, in which he had hit hard on the fact that the next President would determine by his Supreme Court appointments whether recent advances would be wiped out. I complimented him on that and on how the delegates had cheered him.

We talked, then, of Adlai Stevenson and about how, though he had not been elected, he had died one of America's most honored public men because he had spoken out forthrightly on the issues, had pointed the way for America, and had served to help keep the country from going into the dark ages of reaction at a time when, among other things, grown men trembled when the late Senator Joseph McCarthy spoke.

"I don't have to be President, and I may not be," I remember the Vice-President saying, taking strength from his own words. "But I'm going to do the right thing, and I'm going to say what needs to be said."

Pandering to the baser fears and prejudices that lurk within us all is not what Presidents are for. Officials and candidates—and political parties—have a higher duty, a duty to lead, to search out and gather up and shout forth a better vision of ourselves. We do not only need someone to tell us what we look like when we are at our worst. We need someone to help us see what we can be when we are at our best.

That is what is most wrong with the Phillips doctrine and anything like it: it is immoral.

No party can turn its back on black people or the problems of the central cities; no party can refuse to stand up for the poor and hungry without calling into serious question its reason for existing as a political party.

Further, it is important to note—and it is not a mere coincidence—that Vice-President Humphrey began to go up in the polls after his Salt Lake City speech in which he took a stronger stand for peace in Vietnam.

When you are right it rings true. "More important than winning the election is governing the nation. That is the test of a political party—the acid, final test," Adlai Stevenson said in accepting the Democratic nomination at Chicago in 1952, and, while it may not be technically true, as Thomas Jefferson said, that "One man with courage is a majority," he will eventually win over the majority if he is right. If one questions that, he questions whether our system will really work and whether people are smart enough and decent enough to govern themselves.

CHAPTER III

GETTING IT TOGETHER

To say that a Republican conservative coalition strategy will not work, and should not work, is not to say that the other major party, the Democratic Party, will automatically, then, be the majority party. It is not that easy.

There are those who feel that parties in this new age of direct and immediate communications will now cease to exist. In one sense they may have ceased to exist long ago. A political party in America cannot limit its membership or expel a member, nor can it enforce its dogmas on those elected under its banner.

George Washington devoted a substantial portion of his Farewell Address to advice against party factions. "The common and continued mischiefs of the spirit of party," he said, "are sufficient to make it in the interest and duty of a wise people to discourage and restrain it." A good many other early American leaders also opposed parties and thought them unnecessary to the newly formed system of government. Many today would agree, and some expect parties to give way to coalitions around *ad hoc* issues or personalities, or at the very least to a profusion of political parties.

There is room for questioning whether groups formed around a personality will not nearly always limit their own political life to his, whether a minority group or party formed around a single issue or a few issues—though some of these have often been highly effective in selling their ideas—can maintain a strong enough base of power over time for a continuing effect on government, and whether a coalition government made up of minority parties is likely to produce the stability necessary for bold and decisive action.

Sir Henry Sumner Maine wrote in 1886 that "The best historical justification which can be offered for [a system of political parties] is that it has often enabled portions of the nation, who would otherwise be armed enemies, to be only factions."

Professor Harold Laski saw political parties as "the most solid obstacles we have against the danger of Caesarism," and A. L. Lowell, writing in 1913, said that "Their essential function in any democracy and the true reason for their existence is bringing public opinion to a focus and framing issues for the popular verdict."

Popular government and political parties are the alternative to government by force and the transfer of power through violence. The two principal political parties in America already exist—they need not be constructed. They have shown themselves rather durable distilleries for, from time to time, making majorities and for originating—perhaps more often plagiarizing—ideas and popularizing them.

There is indeed, then, important work for the Democratic Party to perform. For, as Professor Alexander M. Bickel of Yale has written, "Majorities do not arise automatically and are not found; they must be constructed and then maintained."

But what is the Democratic Party? In England, power is rightly said to rest in the Parliament. In America, on the other hand, the right to exercise political power has been split up in every direction. The President of the United States is the principal spokesman for his own party, but who speaks for the party which does not occupy the White House? There is *no* official spokesman for the party out of the White House, which is to say that there are a great many: the National Chairman, the leaders of the House and the Senate, the standardbearer of the preceding Presidential campaign (the "titular head of the party") and, as the time for the next Presidential campaign each four years draws nearer, those who are likely or possible Presidential candidates.

Matters are further complicated by the fact that the government of the Democratic Party between conventions is unrepresentative, each state, no matter how large or small, being entitled to two members on the National Committee, and the State Chairmen, who generally must be looked to to carry out decisions made by the National Committee, having no official voice or vote at the national level.

Where do the Democratic governors fit in? This is a question which was brought to my attention quickly and vigorously by Democratic governors soon after I became National Chairman. Governors, with reason, have felt left out of national Party decisions and Party policy in recent years.

Democratic leaders of the House and Senate feel that they are as near to being the "government in exile" as there is one in the American system. They feel that how they and the Democrats in the Congress perform will largely determine the Party's fortunes, especially when Democrats are in a majority in both houses of the Congress. Their specific political goal is the immediate one of electing and re-electing Democratic Congressmen and Senators each two years. Congressional leadership positions and committee chairmanships will be held by Democrats if members who call themselves Democrats or those who vote with them are in the majority; numbers, not ideology, make the difference.

Various unofficial and informal groups and interested individuals—organized labor, Americans for

Democratic Action, minority groups—have a claim on the interest and attention of the Democratic Party, but no formal way is provided for their positions officially to be recognized and represented.

How can these officials, elements, and groups be held together when the situation can hardly be described? As a matter of fact, the mere attempt at definition, of putting things in their place, of graphing it all out neatly in an organization chart, would ignite incredibly explosive arguments. It is very much like the difficulty today's physicists have in observing certain phenomena without changing them by the very act of observation.

The American political system is a true mystery. As David Reisman wrote in *The Lonely Crowd,* "Power in America seems to be situational and mercurial; it resists attempts to locate it in the way a molecule, under the Heisenberg principle, resists attempts simultaneously to locate it and time its velocity."

While I certainly cannot agree with Finley Peter Dunne's Mr. Dooley, who cheerfully declared, "The Democratic Party is never so good as when it is broke, when respectable people speak of it in whispers and when it has no leaders and only one principle—to go in and take it away from the other fellows," I believe it still has an important role to play.

It must keep watch and keep score on the incumbent Republican Administration. It must generate new ideas and propose new solutions. It must call attention to the new problems and help create the climate within which its ideas and solutions can be adopted. And it must serve as the catalyst for the coalition-building process which can produce a majority for those ideas and solutions.

Once, at a meeting with Democratic governors, an influential and intelligent Southern governor took me to task because, he said, the Democratic National Committee was not carrying on more "nuts-and-bolts" activities. He and the other Democratic governors were thereafter impressed, I think, by my report of what we had been able to accomplish in the way of political research, opinion polling and analysis, and other such service-type functions we were performing and planning. I discovered later, however, that what he really meant was that such nuts-and-bolts activities should be the *only* activities the Democratic National Committee carried on. "We need to unite," he said, "and too many of these issues just divide us."

I do not agree with that strategy. Neither did the most controversial and most effective Democratic Chairman of modern times, the late Paul Butler, who served in that capacity when President Eisenhower was in the White House. Mr. Butler and his Democratic Advisory Council, which took positions on issues, were generally in a running public battle with the then leaders of the Senate and House, Lyndon Johnson and Sam Rayburn, who felt the National Committee was infringing on their powers and taking positions which were too liberal.

Adlai Stevenson, who had been the nominee of the

Party, agreed with Mr. Butler. "To be an effective opposition the Democratic Party must have a broader base than the Democrats in Congress," he said. "There are lots of Democratic governors, mayors, officials, leaders and workers around the country who must be informed about Party policy at the national level."

Unity is not possible in the abstract. I believe that people have too many other things to do with their time and money which appeals to them more than getting involved with an organization that does not believe in anything.

That attitude, however, is not universally accepted. And it is not calculated to make life easy for a Party chairman whose job already makes him the usual and most visible target for much of the bitterness and frustration which always lurks within a party that has just lost an election.

"I have been told that the sole duty of the National Chairman is to maintain the unity of the Party," Paul Butler said. "The Chairman, in this view, should behave like the proverbial good child, to be seen and not heard. Unity is a pretty word and I am all for it, but what does it mean? Does it mean unity without regard to conviction, without regard to the ideals which always have been the lifeblood of this Party?"

Then Mr. Butler set forth clearly the course the Democratic Party, in my view, should follow: "I have tried to make the National Committee a clearing-house for the ideas which we as a responsible people must champion or, failing, perish as human beings.

I have seen it as our duty to listen to the many voices of all Democrats, of citizens who know that when they catch our ear they catch the official ear of our Party. I have seen it our duty to express their views as widely and vigorously as we can. I have assumed as an obligation of the Democratic National Committee, not the mere maintenance of unity, but rather a renewed dedication to principle. Unity is founded upon principles rather than upon men."

The first task facing the Democratic Party in 1969 was the need to knit together the threads of communication, so that the Party could begin to speak with some minimum authority and clarity on the basic issues of principle.

Joint meetings of the Democratic National Committee and the Democratic State Chairmen were instituted. A beginning was made toward regular meetings between the Democratic leadership in the Congress and the Democratic governors under the aegis of the Democratic National Committee. A Democratic Policy Council was appointed to speak out on the issues for the Democratic National Committee.

At the insistence of liberal Democrats in the House, the House Democratic caucus began to meet regularly to discuss and take positions on legislation. Senate Majority Leader Mike Mansfield of Montana tried to guide the Senate Democratic Policy Committee toward becoming a true policy-making arm of the Democrats in the Senate. And diplomatic relations were reestablished for the first time in years between the

House and Senate Democratic Campaign Committees and the Democratic National Committee.

Communication was not the only problem the Democratic Party faced. As 1969 began, hostilities and suspicions, many of them earned, were the major features of the political landscape. Retrospective labeling was often the crucial test and final word: "I was for Kennedy; he was for McCarthy; and she was for Humphrey." Sometimes this labeling process was refined even further: "Sure, he was for McCarthy, but not until after the death of Senator Kennedy."

Miss Olga Gechas, who left UNICEF in late 1969 to head the direct-mail solicitation program for the Democratic National Committee, said that she had never known mail to "talk back" as much as the Democratic Party's mail at first did. Democratic solicitation letters she sent out asking for contributions at first resulted in an extremely high percentage of hostile and angry responses. Subtly, month by month, this type of response became less common. The answers became more positive, and the contributions began to increase.

This change in attitude evidenced by the mail reflected a similar change in attitude of Democrats generally toward their Party. There were two or three apparent reasons for this favorable shift in Democratic opinion.

"Idle minds are the devil's workshop," Mother used to say. So long as Democrats had little to do except to continue to dwell upon the disturbing events of the

immediate past, little healing took place and coopera-
tion was out of the question. This came as Democrats
faced concrete situations together. The Democratic
National Committee began to push for Party reform.
Issues such as excessive military spending began to
emerge. The campaigns of such Democratic candidates as David Obey in Wisconsin and Michael Har-
rington in Massachusetts, both of whom were elected
to Congress in special elections in 1969, furnished opportunities for welding together vigorous coalitions of
various Party elements. In all these ways Democrats
began to learn again the importance of trying to work
together.

The passage of time, too, was itself helpful. But,
more important, as the Nixon policies, or lack of them,
began to become apparent, Democrats more and more
were reminded of what had brought them together
in the first place. The underlying reasons for the old
coalitions and traditional alliances which had served
in the past to make the Democrats a majority party,
however strained they might be, were still found to
have some remaining strength. President Nixon's inaugural slogan, "Bring us together," was exactly what
his Supreme Court appointments, legislative recommendations, economic philosophy, and spending priorities began to do for the Democrats.

"He that wrestles with us strengthens our nerves
and sharpens our skill," Edmund Burke once said.
"Our antagonist is our helper."

CHAPTER IV

THE CHOICE IS REFORM
OR DEATH

"**D**eny them this participation of freedom, and you break that sole bond, which originally made, and must still preserve the unity of the empire," Edmund Burke said of the American colonies.

He might well have been speaking of the less powerful members of the Democratic Party. For if the Democratic Party is to hold together as the true and representative instrument of a positive majority in America, it must be made more democratic.

Two overriding issues dominated the chaotic days of the Democratic National Convention in August 1968—how far the Party would go in urging the nation to reverse its course in Vietnam, and, equally pro-

48

found and divisive, how many of the obviously undemocratic procedures for choosing Convention delegates and for running the Convention itself would be
overturned or reformed. These two deep concerns
were inextricably bound together in the minds of
most delegates, regardless of the candidates they
favored for President.

Party reform became an organized issue on August
4, 1968, just prior to the Democratic Convention, when
an *ad hoc* Commission on the Democratic Selection of
Presidential Nominees was formed, primarily by those
who had been active in the preconvention efforts of
Senator Eugene McCarthy and the late Senator Robert
F. Kennedy. Harold Hughes, then Governor and now
Senator from Iowa, was Chairman of the Commission,
the membership of which included Congressman
Donald Fraser of Minnesota, State Representative
Julian Bond of Georgia, Harry Ashmore, Director of
the Center for the Study of Democratic Institutions,
Yale Law School Professor Alexander Bickel, Wash-
ington and California attorney Fred Dutton, and Mrs.
Doris Fleeson Kimball of Washington, D.C.

"This Convention is on trial," the Hughes Commission stated in its report, "The Democratic Choice,"
issued just before the Convention met. "To an extent
not matched since the turn of the twentieth century,
events in 1968 have called into question the integrity
of the convention system for nominating presidential
candidates. Recent developments have put the future
of the two-party system itself into serious jeopardy."

"The crisis of the Democratic Party is a genuine crisis for democracy in America and especially for the two-party system," the report continued. "Racial minorities, the poor, the young, members of the upper-middle class, and much of the lower-middle classes as well—all are seriously considering transferring their allegiance away from either of the two major parties.

"State systems for selecting delegates to the National Convention and the procedures of the Convention itself, display considerably less fidelity to basic democratic principles than a nation which claims to govern itself can safely tolerate."

What could be so terribly wrong, some asked, with a Presidential nominating system that had produced a Woodrow Wilson, a Franklin Roosevelt, an Adlai Stevenson, and a John F. Kennedy? A great deal was wrong, in fact, but it took the crisis of Chicago to make most of us see and understand. As Senator George McGovern has written, "The war exposed the profound flaws in the American Convention system. It showed institutions which work satisfactorily in times considered normal may be unequal to periods of stress. . . . Feelings about the war ran so deep that it became impossible to hide the presence of a fundamental defect within the structure of the Convention system itself. The defect was a failure of democracy, and went to the heart of the American political system."

In a great many ways, the procedure for choosing Convention delegates had made the 1968 and earlier

Conventions undemocratic, unresponsive to ordinary Democrats at the local level, and, in a word, illegitimate. In Georgia, perhaps the most autocratic example of all, Party rules had allowed the state Chairman to choose all delegates to the National Convention, subject only to the Governor's veto. In Louisiana, the Governor had nominated the entire slate of Convention delegates—which, following tradition, was then ratified as a matter of formality by the state committee.

All of the delegates from six states and one of the territories, and parts of another eighteen delegations had been named outright by state Party officials. In many states those officials themselves had been handpicked by the Governor or state Chairman, or, if they had been elected by rank-and-file Party members, had taken office several years before.

A major reform issue had involved the "unit rule," a device which had been used for more than a century in local, state, and National Conventions of the Democratic Party and by which all the votes of a delegation could be compelled to be cast unanimously for a position or candidate favored by the majority of the delegation.

In 1968 the unit rule, in one form or another, had been imposed in Party meetings in fifteen states in such a way as to deny representation, at the next-higher level caucus or convention, to delegates pledged to a particular Presidential candidate. Most frequently this operated to deny delegates favoring Senator Mc-

Carthy a voice at higher stages of the selection process, but in a few instances—for example, in precinct caucuses in Minneapolis and St. Paul, Minnesota—Democrats committed to Vice-President Humphrey had been nearly all denied a voice at the next level because advocates of Senator McCarthy had been in the majority and had claimed the full vote.

Some supporters of Vice-President Humphrey saw the reform movement as nothing more than a maneuver of those who supported other candidates for President. Senator Mondale and I had earlier, for example, publicly called for a prohibition against use of the unit rule in the 1968 Convention, but later, after the Convention had begun, we had found much to our dismay that a member of Vice-President Humphrey's staff had nevertheless assured several Southern governors that this announcement could be compromised. Some of the governors had been rightly angered by this seeming duplicity; others had been puzzled by the confusing statement on this subject which had thereafter emanated from the Humphrey camp. Senator Mondale and I had stuck to our guns.

The larger question of "fair representation" had also become a matter of concern in 1968 in connection with "winner-take-all" primaries and in the appointment of at-large delegates by state Party officials in convention states.

Another common, clear-cut abuse had arisen from the fact that, as late as April 1969, ten state parties had had no written rules whatever. Thus, not only had the very existence of a Democratic Party in those states been determined only by the force of tradition and the wishes of whoever happened to hold office at the time, but the crucial procedures by which convention delegates were selected had also been subject to change from one Presidential election year to the next. There had been strong complaints also about inability to get copies of rules where they existed, failure to make public announcements of meetings, and the use of proxy voting. Slatemaking in both convention and primary states had the effect, though unintended in some cases, of denying an effective voice to the average Democrat.

A fundamental defect in the representative nature of the 1968 Democratic National Convention was the low number of blacks and other minorities, women, and young people, a defect particularly unconscionable because—as one of the best political rhetoricians of our time, Adam Walinsky, recently put it—"This party is the only major vehicle of peaceful political change in the United States. It is the only hope of that kind of change for the poor and the black, for the dreamer and the creator and the young."

Blacks, constituting 12 per cent of the American population and an even higher percentage of the total vote for the Democratic Presidential nominee in the 1964 and 1968 general elections, had made up only 5½ per cent of the delegates to the 1968 Democratic National Convention.

Women comprise more than half of the voting-age

population, yet they made up only 13 per cent of the delegates to the 1968 Convention. The state delegations in 1968 had included so few women that they could not even fill the positions on four standing Convention committees reserved for a woman from each state delegation. Of 118 delegates from Illinois, only eight had been women, and only six of 116 Ohio delegates had been women.

Moreover, in spite of their crucial influence on Presidential politics in 1968, and in spite of the fact that half of the total population of the nation is now under twenty-five years old, young people had been almost totally absent from delegations to the 1968 Convention. Thirteen delegates had included only one person each under thirty, and another sixteen delegations had no voting members at all under thirty.

Forty per cent of the Democratic delegates in 1968 had incomes over $20,000 and only 13 per cent had incomes under $10,000. Poor people had been effectively excluded from becoming delegates in some state by filing fees charged by state parties for entering delegate-selection primaries and by assessments made on delegates once they had been chosen. Too, delegates generally had to pay their own expenses to the National Convention and while in attendance at it.

In addition to these manifestly unfair, undemocratic practices in the delegate-selection process, a great many people had rightly felt, and continue to feel today, that a state's voting strength on the crucial com-

mittees of the National Convention—especially the
Rules, Credentials, and Platform committees—as well
as on the floor of the Convention itself, should be pro-
portionate either to the population of the state, the
number of Democratic voters or registrants, or some
combination of both. Yet, under the rules still in force,
each state delegation, regardless of size, has two members on each of the Convention committees.

Obviously, this size disparity, inconsistent with the
principle of "one man, one vote," is built into the
composition of the National Committee itself, which
consists of two members, a man and a woman, from
each of the fifty states, the District of Columbia, and
the four territories, regardless of population.

Lastly, an excessive concern with security, which
kept thousands of observers and demonstrators miles
distant from the Convention, together with the often
inordinate force used by the Chicago police in disper-
sing and arresting demonstrators, bystanders, delegates, and newsmen alike, exacerbated an already po-
tentially inflammatory situation and heightened the
image of the Convention as one which was rigged and
undemocratic.

Given all the barriers to a truly representative Convention, it is remarkable that the 1968 Convention
nevertheless took strong positions and adopted important resolutions which laid the groundwork for the
reform efforts now well under way in the Party.

The Convention abolished the use of the unit rule
at any stage in the delegate-selection process and it

made clear that delegates, however selected, should be chosen in the same year as the National Convention. It directed the creation of new commissions to further reform the rules and processes of the Party.

When I was elected Democratic National Chairman in January 1969 I was determined that my first important official action would be the appointment of these commissions, because no task seemed more important five months after the Chicago Convention, and three months after the loss of the Presidency, than to begin immediately the process of demonstrating that the Democratic Party intended to keep faith with the decisions made in Chicago and was capable of fundamental reform from within.

It would be hard for one who was not involved to imagine the depth of feeling with which so many Democrats continued to fight for reform. "What is there left out of all this horrible year that we can still work for?" one intense lady asked me. Her emotional commitment and the similar commitment of others like her were eloquent testimony to their hopes for the Party and the system.

On the same day I was elected Chairman, the Democratic National Committee passed two resolutions, reaffirming the mandates for reform and directing the appointment of a Commission on Party Structure and Delegate Selection and a Commission on Rules to carry them out.

Senator George McGovern's willingness to head the Commission on Party Structure and Delegate Selection was convincing evidence to many that the Party was serious about reform, and Congressman James O'Hara of Michigan, as Chairman of the Rules Commission, added stature to the work of that important group.

Wisely, the McGovern Commission embarked immediately upon a series of sixteen hearings all around the country, taking the testimony of nearly 500 witnesses, their goal being summed up well by the Reverend Channing Phillips, Democratic National Committeeman from the District of Columbia, who said: "In the year 1968, many of the Democrats of the District went through a fascinating experience in open democracy, not only because we had a primary, but because a serious effort was made to involve every neighborhood, every citizen in that primary; and because a serious effort was made to discuss issues. The net result was that the elected State delegation and Central Committee was and is a beautiful cross-section of the District, ranging from a millionaire to a welfare recipient, from black and white militants to more conservative Democrats. Such heterogeneity ought to be the hallmark of the Democratic Party across our country, truly a party of the people."

On the same day I appointed the two national reform commissions, I also called upon the Chairman of each state party to appoint his own statewide reform commission. The response was most encouraging. By the spring of 1970, more than thirty states had set up one or more such reform groups, and many had achieved significant progress in adopting reform measures on their own. The Michigan Democratic Party, for example, held a statewide reform convention, attended by 2000 delegates, at which Party processes were completely modernized. The North Carolina Democratic Party adopted progressive changes proposed by its reform commission. The Minnesota Democratic-Farmer-Labor Party agreed to a new and more democratic party constitution. Several state legislatures, including those in Rhode Island, Maryland, and Illinois, enacted new state laws, at the urging of Democrats, to guarantee far greater voter participation in the delegate-selection process.

Following its hearings, the McGovern Commission completed an intensive study of the delegate-selection process in every state and territory and then issued official guidelines for the states to follow to effect the necessary reforms.

During this same period, the O'Hara Commission held hearings on the rules of the Democratic National Committee, convention arrangements and rules, the role of media at the convention, and the rules of convention committees. Among its most helpful witnesses was Congressman Donald Fraser of Minnesota, who stated, "The major new trust ... should be in the direction of creating a more genuinely *national* Democratic Party. By this I mean that we should firmly set our course away from the tradition of 50 state parties, each autonomous within a poorly-defined, national confederation, meeting every four years to nominate

a presidential candidate. We should set as our goal
the creation of a truly national party in which decision-
making at the national level is strengthened and the
50 state parties become integral parts of that party."

Other witnesses made additional suggestions for
improving the way conventions are run. Many felt,
as I do, for example, that the more than 5000 delegates
and alternates who were sent to the Chicago Convention in 1968 were just too many, for as James Madison
wrote, ". . . in all legislative assemblies the greater the
number composing them may be, the fewer will be
the men who will in fact direct the proceedings."

As I made clear in my statement of resignation to
the Democratic National Committee, reform is of fundamental importance to the future of the Democratic
Party. It must come, and quickly, while the state legislatures still have time to act prior to 1972, before reform questions become entangled again with the Presidential politics of the next Convention and before
the passion for reform is eroded by new issues.

Reform must become reality because, if the Democratic Party is to remain the majority party, it must
demonstrate to those essential to its coalition that the
processes by which the Party nominates for the Presidency and makes all its other decisions not only allow
but also encourage the widest involvement by them.
In no other way can they be persuaded that the Democratic Party truly represents them and their views on
the critical issues which face the country.

But passive changes in the rules, important as they

are, will not be sufficient. With new life styles and living patterns, neither the clubhouse nor the precinct meeting attracts sufficient participation. That is why, during the time I served as Chairman of the Democratic National Committee, new efforts were launched to encourage more black people and women, for example, to run for office. A new consumer action project was started to engage women, particularly, in action on this issue at the local level, a prototype for the kinds of program which I believe the Party must sponsor in the field of social action to give more people a chance to *do* something about issues and not just to *say* something about them. We joined with the new President of the Young Democrats, David Sternoff, in planning to revitalize the Youth Division of the Party and to help it toward building an action corps of young people throughout the country—not necessarily requiring them to sign in blood that they would always support Democrats—organized around fundamental issues, such as the Vietnam war, the environment, the eighteen-year-old vote, and implementation of the McGovern Commission recommendations.

"In the past, when political parties have had a choice between reform and a quiet death, they have almost invariably chosen death," Senator McGovern said recently. "The Democratic Party seems to have undertaken to choose reform and life."

I hope that is so. There have been some recent expressions of misgivings by Senator Eugene McCarthy and others as to whether the present Party leaders will carry forward the reforms which have been charted and begun. They must.

Looking back at the 1968 Democratic Convention and campaign and looking forward to 1972, some things seem very clear to me.

No man will be nominated by the Democrats and elected President in 1972 who has not entered and proved himself in the earlier primaries.

This is a good development for three reasons. First, as a practical matter, the man who seeks his Party's nomination for President should be required to show without doubt that he has genuine popular appeal, that he is electable.

Second, campaigns improve candidates. A hard-fought campaign requires a man to face up to the issues that really concern people and more distinctly to define and state his own thinking on them. Candidates become more capable of filling an office by what they learn in the very act of campaigning for it.

Third, campaigns improve voters. John J. Gilligan, the progressive new Democratic Governor of Ohio, made a very impressive but unsuccessful campaign for the Senate in that state in 1968, stressing his anti-war views. Though unsuccessful then, his campaign nevertheless served to change the climate considerably in Ohio on that and other issues. Benefiting from this improved climate, which he had principally helped to create, Mr. Gilligan was elected Governor two years later. And, interestingly enough, the man who beat him for the Senate in 1968, Senator William Saxbe, a

Republican, turned out to be more dovish on the Vietnam war and more progressive on many domestic issues than most Ohio Republicans would have imagined, a fact not unrelated to the changed political climate in his home state.

Thus it is important that there continue to be a scattering of preferential primaries prior to the Democratic National Convention to allow both a sampling and an educating of Democratic sentiment and to require a testing of candidate appeal. I would not be surprised to see as many as ten or twelve Presidential aspirants enter the 1972 Democratic primaries. Senator Eugene McCarthy of Minnesota was not very well known throughout the country until he garnered 40 per cent of the vote and a great deal of the spotlight in the New Hampshire primary of 1968. Similarly, the early 1972 primaries could very well cause one or more national figures to emerge within the Democratic Party almost overnight.

The National Convention should not be replaced by a national primary. To do so would further restrict the ranks of those who could run for President to the wealthy and the friends of the wealthy; the costs would be enormous. Further, a national primary could not replace the coalition-building and platform-writing functions of the Party Convention.

But no man will be elected President in 1972 who begins the campaign as the nominee of a Democratic National Convention which a substantial number of Democrats can legitimately charge has not been truly representative and democratic. The Convention does not have to be a tranquil one for its nominee to win—and probably will not be. But there must be a feeling on the part of all those taking part in it—and, more importantly, in the minds of the people of the nation watching it on television—that the delegates actually speak for the nation's Democrats. If a substantial minority leaves the 1972 Democratic Convention believing and being able to charge with some justification that the Convention was unrepresentative and undemocratic, the Party's nominee might as well go on home and forget it.

That is why I think Party reform is essential. That is why I made it the primary object of my chairmanship of the Democratic Party, despite the fact that during the early months of these beginning efforts toward reform it was a divisive issue within the Party.

Popular control of the people's Party is a prerequisite to government truly responsive to the people's needs. The Democratic Party should live up to what it calls itself.

CHAPTER V

LET THE PEOPLE RULE

"If liberty and equality, as is thought by some, are chiefly to be found in democracy," Aristotle wrote more than two thousand years ago, "they will be best attained when all persons alike share in the government to the utmost."

That, I believe, is still a true statement of the democratic ideal, but we are a long way yet from making it reality in America, and in some ways we are going backward. It will do no good to reform political parties unless the result is reform of the government. That is what is important.

In 1876, 82 per cent of men over the age of twenty-one cast ballots in the Presidential election, but, only 60 per cent of the population of voting age came to the polls in 1968. That meant that eight million more potential voters stayed away from the polls in 1968 than did four years earlier, in the 1964 Presidential election. Only thirty million people voted for Mr. Nixon in 1968; forty-seven million potential voters—seventeen million more—did not bother to vote at all.

While it may not be strictly true that "All the ills of democracy can be cured by more democracy," as Alfred E. Smith once said, that statement does point the way we must go.

In some countries the law requires that those who can read and write *must* vote. Strangely, in America, where we pay homage to the democratic ideal, we place all sorts of legal obstacles in the way of voting.

If we really believe in democracy in this country, we must assure every citizen's freedom to vote. If we really believe in citizen participation, we must knock down the unreasonable barriers which still restrict it.

If the rights of the people are to be safeguarded, we must eliminate the obvious and remaining unreasonable restrictions against popular participation in government, including the insupportable restrictions based upon age, color, and residency, as well as the undemocratic Electoral College machinery and illogical voter-registration requirements, all of which work to thwart the will of the people.

Young people today are maturing, both physically and intellectually, at far earlier ages than ever before. Through television and improved education, a young person today becomes aware at an early age of the

real world and the problems of the real world; he becomes concerned about these problems and rightly
wants to be involved in solving them. We must recognize this fact and respond to it.

The newest generation of Americans is the largest,
best-educated, and most dedicated group of young
people our nation has ever produced. In 1940, 40 per
cent of our population was under twenty-five. Today,
the proportion is 47 per cent, and by 1972 over half
of the American population will be under twenty-five.
The number of Americans entering college has increased by fully one-third since 1960.

In early 1970, the Congress decided that it could
by statute, under the Fourteenth Amendment to the
Constitution, give the right to vote in all elections—
local, state, and federal—to eighteen-year-olds. In this
it agreed with Professor Archibald Cox of Harvard
Law School, former Solicitor General, who testified
before a Senate Committee that the Supreme Court
decision in the case of *Morgan* v. *Katzenbach,* which
held that Congress has broad powers to legislate in
regard to voting qualifications under the "equal protection" clause of the Constitution, ". . . did recognize
fully the power of the Congress to make this determination with respect to voting age, and to change the
age limit by statute."

President Nixon signed the bill with some publicly
stated misgivings about its constitutionality, and procedures were begun for an early court test. Though
the Supreme Court ruled in favor of the lower age for

federal elections only, an overwhelming majority of the members of both houses of Congress had recognized the right of eighteen-year-olds to vote, and there should be no stopping of the full implementation of this right by constitutional amendment.

There has been a great change in the age at which young people take jobs, get married, and raise families. Four states—Georgia since 1943, Kentucky since 1955, and Alaska and Hawaii since they entered the Union in 1959—granted the right to persons under twenty-one to vote without any resultant difficulty—rather, indeed, with generally acclaimed success.

Many of the arguments which have been used against the right of eighteen-year-olds to vote were used in the resistance to women's suffrage more than fifty years ago; they are no longer acceptable.

As Senator Edward Kennedy of Massachusetts said in support of the statutory change which he and the Majority Leader of the Senate, Mike Mansfield of Montana, proposed, 30 per cent of our forces in Vietnam and one-half of those who have died there are under twenty-one years of age. "They have earned the right to vote," he said, "and they can counsel us wisely at the polls."

America needs the energy, enthusiasm, and idealism of young people as full participants in our political system, and there is no more basic way by which that involvement can be encouraged than by opening up to them the full right of participation at the ballot box.

Historically, the greatest bar to voting in our country

has been color. The Voting Rights Act of 1965 was the most effective civil rights legislation ever passed. Under its provisions, requiring the federal government to take affirmative action by sending examiners and inspectors into the Southern states, more than 800,000 additional black voters were registered to vote and more than 400 black candidates were elected to public office. Today, as Howard A. Glickstein, Staff Director of the U.S. Commission on Civil Rights, has testified, "Significant numbers of moderate white officials hold office because white and black voters have been able to turn out of office the Jim Clarks and the Bull Conners in many communities. This is what the right to vote is all about; the people have the right to determine who will govern and represent them."

The Congress in 1970, rejecting recommendations of the Nixon Administration for relaxation of this highly successful law, voted overwhelmingly for its extension, impressed by the testimony of such witnesses as Vernon E. Jordan, Jr., then Director of the Voter Education Project of the Southern Regional Council, who graphically predicted what would have resulted from failure to do so when he said: "I know as well as any man in this room that Canton and Grenada and Selma and Sandersville and hundreds of other Southern communities stand poised and ready to eliminate the burgeoning black vote in their jurisdiction. The slightest flicker of a green light from Washington is all these white-dominated communities need. When they receive the signal, they will act."

Despite the recommendations of President Nixon to the contrary, no such regressive signal came from Washington, and Congress made it clear that there was to be no retreat from the front lines in the fight for the basic right to vote to which black people had so recently advanced.

As a part of its landmark decision to extend the Voting Rights Act of 1965, the Congress decided to go two steps further and strike down residency and literacy requirements because it was felt that, in a highly mobile society and one in which television is in almost universal use, such requirements were unnecessary and improper abridgments of the right of suffrage.

Father Theodore M. Hesburgh, President of Notre Dame University and Chairman of the U.S. Commission on Civil Rights, made the case against residency requirements which, it is reliably estimated, disenfranchised more than five million people otherwise eligible to vote in the 1968 Presidential election. He stated in a letter to President Nixon: "Residency requirements seem unreasonable when applied to presidential elections, for which familiarity with local issues and personalities is irrelevant. The Commission is especially concerned because the burden of such requirements falls heavily on migrant workers, mainly Mexican-Americans from the Southwest, who are often unable to vote either in their home state or in the state in which they are working."

The Congress rightly agreed with a similar argument against literacy tests, wherever they were applied. "We found that literacy tests do have a negative effect on voter registration, and that this impact of literacy tests falls most heavily on blacks and persons of Spanish surname," Howard Glickstein of the U.S. Civil Rights Commission testified. "Particularly persons for whom English is not a native language are intimidated by the prospect of the test and fear the embarrassment of failing it or, where the test consists of reading a text aloud, of mispronouncing words."

It is time to move also against the outmoded Electoral College. In 1907, at statehood, Thomas P. Gore and Robert L. Owen were elected as the first United States Senators to represent the newly recognized State of Oklahoma. Actually, Thomas P. Gore had received only the *third* highest number of votes cast in the preceding statewide Senatorial referendum, but a gentleman's agreement had been made at the Oklahoma Constitutional Convention by which the two halves of the new state, east and west, would each have one of the first two Senators. This gentleman's agreement could be, and was, carried into effect because the statewide referendum had no legal standing, since in that day U.S. Senators were elected not by the people but by the state legislature. This procedure, instituted by those who mistrusted popular rule, seems foreign to us now. It would never be countenanced today and would be denounced, were it advocated, as outrageously undemocratic.

Yet American citizens still do not have the right to elect their own President and Vice-President. Instead,

citizens of each state are allowed by their votes to
select electors, and these electors are permitted then
to cast the votes of each state, not even being required
in most states to vote in accordance with the majority
will. Worse, if there is no majority of Electoral College
votes in the country, the selection of the President is
decided by the U.S. House of Representatives.

Once it became clear in the wee hours following
Election Day 1968 that Vice-President Humphrey
would not be chosen President by a majority vote of
the Electoral College, I recall with what dread many
of us contemplated the constitutional crisis which
seemed in prospect if the selection were thrown into
the House of Representatives. One member of the
Vice-President's staff immediately began to draw up
voting lists purporting to predict the House votes
which could be counted upon to be cast for Mr.
Humphrey. "If we can just get one more popular vote
than Nixon gets, we can make a stronger race in the
House," this zealous staffer had already been heard to
say. "But I believe we can win in the House in any
event." The thought was chilling.

The long evolution of popular democracy in America has finally brought the nation to another important
time of decision: whether or not to abolish the Electoral College and give the people the full power directly to elect the President of the United States. There
is common agreement that the present Electoral College system is full of inequities and dangers to our
political stability.

The facts are unarguable. Three times the *runner-up* in the popular vote has been elected President. Using the 1960 census, it takes 392,930 citizens of California to equal the voting power of 75,389 citizens of Alaska in the Electoral College. Under the present "winner-take-all" system, the citizen who votes for the losing candidate in a given state is not only disenfranchised, but also finds his dissenting vote being cast for the winning candidate in the Electoral College. As Thomas Hart Benton said of this archaic system over a century ago, "To lose their votes is the fate of all minorities, and it is their duty to submit; but this is not a case of votes lost, but of votes taken away, added to those of the majority and given to a person to whom the minority is opposed."

In the 1968 election, Vice-President Humphrey was awarded the eight electoral votes of Connecticut by receiving the votes of 616,000 people, while Mr. Nixon picked up an offsetting eight electoral votes in South Carolina when only 261,000 people there voted for him. Where is the justice in that?

Where indeed? The article of our Constitution which sets forth the method by which a President is elected has at long last, through time and radically changed circumstances, finally come into conflict with the fundamental principles upon which our entire system of popular government rests. Direct election of the President is the only method which meets all of the requisite tests. It is the only method which eliminates all inequities.

Some have spoken out against the popular election of Presidents because they say it would destroy the two-party system. I do not agree. The plan advocated by Senator Birch Bayh of Indiana would require a 40 per cent plurality for election, thus encouraging, as Senator Bayh has stated, "potential splinter groups to continue to operate within the framework of the two-party system, since no minor party could reasonably hope to win forty per cent of the total popular vote." Neither am I moved by the argument of some urban spokesmen that direct election would lessen the influence of urban states. Rural opponents of the plan have argued just the opposite. The truth is that, with direct popular election, each person's vote would count the same, and communities of the same size would have the same influence, whether in a large state or a small one, and, as Senator Bayh has made clear, "We ought never to have a privileged class of voters—and certainly not in the election of the President."

The responsibility and the power of the modern American President, nationally as well as internationally, are so awesome, when compared with those when the Electoral College was devised, that it should come as no surprise that the method of choosing a President to govern a slightly populated nation of competing states in the eighteenth century simply will not do today. The President of the United States must now have an electoral mandate that is clearly evident to and understood by people all over the earth. Times have changed, and if we expect to live up to our basic principles, we must eliminate the present constitutional distortion of the popular vote for President and insure beyond reasonable doubt the sovereign power of the people to elect. "If the President is to be the man of the people, if all the people are to stand on the same footing, equal masses of people must be given equal votes, equal bargaining power," noted political economist Lucius Wilmerding, Jr., has correctly said.

Ours is a democratic system of government in which the government derives its powers from the consent of the governed. The people of America know what this means; that is why both the Gallup and Harris polls show that 81 per cent of them favor outright abolition of the Electoral College.

"The Federal system is not strengthened through an antiquated device which has not worked as it was intended to work when it was included in the Constitution and which, if anything, has become a divisive force in the Federal system by pitting groups of states against groups of states," Senator Mike Mansfield of Montana has wisely commented. "The Presidency has evolved, out of necessity, into the principal political office, as the courts have become the principal legal bulwark beyond districts, beyond states, for safeguarding the interests of all the people in all the states. And since such is the case, in my opinion, the Presidency should be subject to the direct and equal control of all the people."

Otis H. Shao, Dean of the Graduate School of the

University of the Pacific, put his finger on another important reason for changing our system for electing Presidents, the difference between what we profess and what we practice, when he said that "those of us who explain the ways of our government to oncoming generations of students and voters find that we become artful dodgers as we attempt to justify the Electoral College.

"To insure the rights of all eligible Americans— young and old, majority and minority groups, urban and rural residents—to have their voting wishes count, we need a direct election of the man who will hold the highest office in the land."

It is outrageous that the archaic filibuster rule of the Senate was used to prevent a 1970 vote on this issue in that body. The fight for this reform is a fundamental one, and it must be continued with renewed determination.

State voter-registration requirements are also undemocratic. Whether or not Senator Ralph Yarborough of Texas could possibly be re-elected in November 1970 was actually first determined many months earlier, in January of that year, when every Texan who expected to take part in that decision had to go to a certain place on a certain day and reregister, as is required annually in that state.

Long before citizen interest in distant elections has been stirred, each prospective voter in Texas must be sufficiently motivated to register to vote, or else he will be ineligible to take part in the vital decisions to be made in the elections which are to follow many months later. Obviously, this kind of legal device especially bars poor whites and Mexican-American, black, and other minority voters in Texas from exerting their full electoral strength in the state. In many other states, the registration laws are almost equally undemocratic.

Organizing and promoting drives to get people registered has always been an extremely costly and wasteful aspect of Democratic campaigns. This essential activity was sadly neglected in the poorly financed 1968 Presidential campaign of Vice-President Humphrey, especially because the registration drive in some states would have had to have been launched and financed even before Mr. Humphrey had secured the nomination of the Convention. These unnecessarily restrictive state laws can and should be liberalized by state legislatures, but uniform national action is what is needed most.

It was because of this particular problem that I appointed the Freedom To Vote Task Force of the Democratic National Committee in 1969 and named as its Chairman and Vice-Chairman former Attorney General Ramsey Clark and Mrs. Mildred Robbins, Honorary President of the National Council of Women. Their job was summed up well in the beginning statement Mr. Clark made: "If you believe in our system of government, you want everybody to participate, and you'll take your chances with the decision."

The Universal Voter Enrollment plan, which the

Ramsey Clark task force recommended, would shift the initial burden of registration from the individual to the federal government. The United States is virtually the only advanced democratic nation in the world which does not have such a plan. The idea is not new and has been found successful in Canada as well as in several of the states. Where used, it has resulted in voter registration of more than 90 per cent of the voting-age population. It is an inexpensive and effective means of shoring up the foundations of our democratic institutions.

Under this plan, in the weeks immediately preceding an election, enrollment officers would visit every residence in the land and enroll to vote every qualified person who does not refuse, much like the taking of the census—and for a far more fundamental purpose.

No citizen would be barred from voting because of failure to enroll before election day, or because of loss of enrollment certificate or absence from his district or from the country. Nor would he be disqualified from voting for President if he changed his place of residence, even on the day before the election. He would in that case simply have to complete an affidavit identifying himself, following a procedure no more complicated than that required to cash a check.

The recommendations of the Ramsey Clark task force would be administered by a National Election Commission and would cost only five million dollars in non-Presidential election years and fifty million in Presidential election years—or less than fifty cents per eligible voter, a small price to pay to allow the involvement of all our citizens in the electoral process.

Elections would be much more fair, because they would be less dependent upon which candidate or party was able to register the greatest number of supporters, as well as turn them out to vote. The public, rather than individual candidates or parties with axes to grind, would pay for the registration of voters—a less costly, because more consolidated, process.

The task force also recommended the establishment of a National Elections holiday on the date of every Presidential election "to assure full opportunity for voter participation and to solemnize this as the most important occasion for the exercise of a citizen's obligations in a free society."

The Congress must become more responsive to the people. Majority caucuses in the Senate and House should meet regularly and publicly, committee chairmen and conference committee members must be made more responsible to the majority, and the seniority rule must cease to work against the public will.

Since the founding of our country, we have amended the Constitution six times to extend the voting power of the people: The Fourteenth and Fifteenth Amendments granted black people the right to vote; the Seventeenth Amendment provided for the direct election of United States Senators; the Nineteenth Amendment allowed women to vote; the Twenty-third Amendment extended voting rights to residents of the District of Columbia; and the Twenty-fourth Amendment made the poll tax illegal. The movement in America has been progressively and inexorably toward more popular control of the government. It is time now to move further in the people's interest.

"This country, with its institutions, belongs to the people who inhabit it," Abraham Lincoln declared. "Why should there not be a patient confidence in the ultimate justice of the people? Is there any better or equal hope in the world?"

There is, indeed, no better or equal hope than a patient confidence in the ultimate justice of the people, if we will remove the remaining and unreasonable barriers to the free expression of their will.

CHAPTER VI

NOT TO
THE HIGHEST BIDDER

"If you look like a winner, your financial worries end in the closing hours of the campaign," the late James Michael Curley, onetime Mayor of Boston, once said. "If you look like a loser, your financial worries begin to mount." The battle-scarred old model for *The Last Hurrah* added candidly: "When I was a loser, it was many weeks and sometimes months before 'the ghost would walk.'"

Following the losing Presidential campaign of 1968, it was a long time before the Democratic ghost would walk.

Abraham Lincoln was said to have been able to return $199.25 of the $200 raised to finance his Congressional campaign of 1846. Campaign costs have increased since then.

Richard Nixon spent about $500,000 in 1960 to get his Party's nomination; in 1968 it cost him more than $10 million. Hubert Humphrey, before dropping out after the West Virginia primary, spent about $250,000 in 1960; in 1968, after a late start and without competing with Senators McCarthy and Kennedy in the costly primaries, he still spent about $4 million prior to the convention. In both parties, all candidates for nomination spent around $40 million prior to the Party conventions.

Thereafter, the Democrats reported expenditures for the 1968 Humphrey-Muskie general election campaign of $13.6 million. The Republicans listed $29.6 million Nixon-Agnew general election expenditures, and former Governor George Wallace's campaign disclosed expenditures of $7.2 million.

Herbert Alexander, Director of the Citizens Research Foundation, which is the source for most of these figures, has estimated that a total of $100 million was spent to elect a President in 1968, including preconvention expenses of all candidates, the cost of the conventions, and the expenses of the general election campaign. Mr. Alexander reports that there were quite a few individual contributions to one or another of the various Presidential candidates as high as the $100,000-to-$500,000 range.

Obviously, the Republican Party had an easier time raising money during the general election campaign than did the Democratic Party. And, being winners, the ease with which the Republicans were able to raise money after the election, to pay their debts and for other purposes, was even more enhanced. The party that occupies the White House discovers that there are a good many people who, for reasons of desired preference or prestige of one kind or another, are more than happy to make contributions to the political party of the President.

It was precisely this kind of good financial fortune during the Democratic Presidential years from 1960 to 1968 that caused a great deal of the financial problems of the Humphrey-Muskie general election campaign and of the Democratic Party thereafter.

Reliable estimates indicate that the Democratic National Committee, which, in the lean years prior to President Kennedy's inauguration in 1960, was 70 per cent dependent upon small contributions, thereafter, during the fat Presidential years which followed, became 70 per cent dependent upon large contributors. Some of these contributors had given money only because of their personal friendship with the man in the White House or because of other personal ties to him and felt no strong obligation to the Party, its 1968 nominees, or specific issues. Others felt they had already done their share through the years and should not be called upon to contribute so much again. And some had little desire to back what the polls indicated, until near the very last, was a campaign almost certain to lose. When, for one or another of these reasons, such large contributions were less available, the Humphrey-Muskie campaign was almost pitifully lacking in the ability to tell its story to the people.

The fund-raising task of the Democrats after the 1968 Convention was not made any easier by the fact that throughout the country there were considerable debts left over from the preconvention efforts. The campaign of the late Senator Robert F. Kennedy was said to be more than $3 million in debt, Vice-President Humphrey and Senator Eugene McCarthy each had incurred unpaid campaign bills of around $1 million, and even Senator George McGovern's late entry had been financed partly on borrowed money.

On top of all that, Vice-President Humphrey's Presidential nomination made him the titular head of a Party which not only had no cash on hand but was, itself, in debt, even owing several hundred thousand dollars for the expenses of the very Convention which, by its awful and divisive nature, had simultaneously given him the nomination and made it almost impossible for him to win the election.

In the weeks and months which followed the Convention, the financial plight of the Democratic Party was so bleak that at one point the campaign staff could not get delivery on the results of vital public opinion polls they had commissioned. This essential information was not available to help plan the campaign strategy because it could not be paid for.

At another point in the campaign, printed campaign materials could not be shipped because the printing costs were not paid, and the materials remained stored for a long time in a warehouse, undistributed. After a few weeks, the Democratic Party had to decide to forego putting out any literature at all, and thereafter whatever printed materials were used were printed locally or independently by labor or other friends of the campaign. Most damaging to the campaign, no exposure was possible on television, the important campaign medium, until very near the very last—and too late.

Vice-President Humphrey and Senator Muskie had to be ingenious in taking advantage of every opportunity for free appearances on television and radio talk shows and in getting newspaper attention. Their efforts alone carried the campaign during its wretched early months. Their efforts and the issues which began to emerge more clearly gave a final lift to the campaign which was reflected at the last in the public opinion polls. Thereafter, the Democratic Party was able to borrow $5 million to finish up the campaign and for a last-minute television appeal. As is always true in a campaign, there was in the closing days of the Humphrey-Muskie campaign in 1968 a kind of "chicken and egg" effect: if the campaign is good, the money comes in; if the money comes in (even though, in this instance, borrowed), the campaign is good.

Vice-President Humphrey had urgently sought to even up the odds somewhat by vigorously and repeatedly demanding that the candidates debate on television, as had been done in 1960. Mr. Nixon steadfastly refused, and this refusal in itself became something of an issue and one which cast Vice-President Humphrey in a more favorable light. Nevertheless, the failure to get public debates between the candidates, given Vice-President Humphrey's financial inability to pay for enough of his own television appearances, proved to be an important factor in the outcome of the election.

Thus, in January 1969, I was elected to preside over a Party which had been defeated and was deeply in debt. Moreover, on the same day I was elected, the Democratic National Committee agreed to assume $2 million of the preconvention debts of Vice-President Humphrey and the late Senator Robert F. Kennedy, hoping thereby to enlist the greater effort of all the various elements in the Party to help pay off the combined Party debts, thus enlarged.

"Victory has many fathers, but defeat is an orphan." Raising money was harder than it had ever been. There was no large group of loyal small contributors upon which the Party could depend, and so we sponsored dinners, galas, and everything else anyone could think of to build a professional staff, to begin some worthwhile activities, and to keep our doors open. I said at one point, quite truthfully, "If the wolf comes to our door, he'll have to bring a picnic lunch."

Most importantly, we decided that if the Democratic Party was actually going to be the "Party of the people," as we liked to boast, it was going to have to build financial participation from a much greater

number of smaller contributors. Only with that kind
of financial base would the Party be able to remain
active in good years and bad and would it be able to
take positions on issues without fearing that its principal
backers would be angered. Accordingly, I hired Miss
Olga Gechas from UNICEF, where she had been
successful in building their direct-mail solicitation program from receipts of $800,000 per year to something
over $5 million. Miss Gechas moved down to Washing-
ton in late 1969 and began a program of testing various
mailing lists and types of appeals on behalf of the
Party. From this small effort, the Party in 1969 received contributions of approximately $300,000, more
than twice the amount received from such sources in
the comparable year of 1967, the average contribution
being $17. It was obvious that the Participating Mem-
bership program could be highly successful if properly
funded.

We discovered that, according to a study made by
the Survey Research Center at the University of Michigan, only 23 per cent of the people had been asked to
make a political contribution in 1968. Most of those who
had been asked had been solicited by the Republicans.
Indeed, we found that the Republican National Committee had over the years built up direct-mail solicitation program to the extent that it had a list of 400,000
contributors who regularly gave an average of $10 per
year to the Party. While it costs a great deal to develop
this kind of financial base, it is essential that the Democratic Party continue the effort we began in 1969, and

I made that strong recommendation to the National Committee at the time I left the Chairmanship. I also recommended that the Party continue efforts which had been begun toward making a nationwide television appeal for funds from small givers, to get away from the old traditional fund-raising methods and to make it more certain by this means, also, that the Democratic Party would be owned by everybody.

These are important programs which must be continued to insure popular control of the Democratic Party in the future, but more fundamental legislative measures are required as well if the interests of the great mass of people are to be protected.

The first time I was a candidate for public office, I was appalled to find that newspapers generally charged a higher rate for political advertisements than they did for regular commercial advertisements. "Political advertising is more risky financially," one editor told me, despite the fact that he then, as is the custom, demanded cash payment in advance. My impression is that most newspapers in Oklahoma have since corrected this practice, but that is not true everywhere.

For example, in early 1970 the Washington *Post* was asked to quote advertising rates for a full-page advertisement seeking funds for black Democratic candidates. In the discussion which ensued, the *Post* advertising department, incredibly, stated that, while Safeway or any other retail advertiser only had to pay $2248.67 for a full-page advertisement during the week and $2520.42 on Sunday, political candidates had to pay for the same full-page space nearly $800 more in each instance, $3040.56 on a weekday and $3287.76 on Sunday! If the Democratic Party wanted to run a full-page advertisement stating, for example, its position on an issue, the cost was even higher. We were told that the same full-page would cost nearly another $800 more, $3831 on a weekday and $4103 on Sunday! Moreover, while it was possible for some retail advertisers to get credit, we learned that candidates or political parties were required to pay cash in advance, even if the advertisement were booked through an advertising agency.

Though democracy can only work if good men stand for public office, we seem to be, more and more, making it appear to be a rich man's game.

The costs of political campaigns are skyrocketing alarmingly. Estimates are that $300 million was spent in all campaigns in 1968, local, state and federal—$100 million more than in 1964 and $160 million more than in 1952. In other words, there was a 50 per cent increase in the cost of campaigns in the four years between 1964 and 1968.

The Federal Communications Commission reported expenditures of $58.9 million for political broadcasting in all campaigns in 1968, a figure more than 70 per cent higher than was spent for that purpose in 1964.

A Senatorial campaign in a state where an expenditure of $250,000 was considered adequate six years ago must now consider budgets upward of $1 million, and Senator John Pastore of Rhode Island stated to the

Senate in 1970 that he had noted reports that it cost $10 million to run for Governor of New York and that one candidate for Mayor of New York City had spent $3 million.

President Dwight Eisenhower called attention to the serious problem posed by these mounting costs in an article he wrote in 1968: "We have put a dollar sign on public service, and today many capable men who would like to run for office simply can't afford to do so. Many believe that politics in our country is already a game exclusively for the affluent. This is not strictly true; yet the fact that we may be approaching that state of affairs is a sad reflection on our elective system."

Appearances are important if there is to be confidence in our system. "Holders of public office should not have to be obligated, or even appear to be obligated, to large contributors who made it possible for them to stand for office," said the late Senator Robert F. Kennedy. "Able young people should not be deterred from entering politics by the fear of having to compromise their values and their independence in order to obtain financing."

The growing threat to our system of popular government which the high cost of campaigning represents moved me to name former Chief of Protocol Lloyd Hand of California and Representative Martha Griffiths of Michigan to head a Campaign Financing Commission of the Democratic National Committee. It was the responsibility of that panel to help improve public awareness of this problem and to make recommendations concerning means of securing the action which the seriousness of the problem urgently requires.

If the rights and powers of the people are to be properly safeguarded in the political process, I believe that we should move at once to allow a tax credit for small contributions to political candidates and parties and to provide each Presidential, Senatorial, and Congressional candidate a minimum amount of television time in the general election at reduced cost.

The revolutionary increase in dependence upon television and the rise in television rates (30 to 40 per cent between 1961 and 1967) are the principal reasons campaign costs have gone up so rapidly in recent years. Of course, postage rates have also gone up, and it costs, for example, more than $300,000 for a candidate to send just one first-class-mail letter to every family in Texas. But, basically, costs have gone up because, as Senator Ernest F. Hollings of South Carolina has stated, 97 per cent of American homes have television sets which are turned on more than five and a half hours a day and, while less than 10 per cent of the people saw any political candidate for any office in person in 1968, 59 per cent of them got their news from television—and the candidate or party that wants to be successful must recognize these facts and make television the prime medium of appeal. One spot of one-minute duration on television can reach twenty-three million people of voting age, one-third of all the votes cast in the 1968 election, yet a one-minute network spot during the popular *Gunsmoke* program costs $50,000 for the time, and more for production.

"Television has become the 20th Century Athenian town square, the modern Roman forum, owned by the people and where they gather for the transaction of mercantile, judicial and political business," Russell D. Hemenway, Director of the National Committee for an Effective Congress, stated in 1970 hearings. "It is where the political contenders go to be heard, and where the citizens' decisions are formed. The airways belong to the public, as the Agora belonged to the Athenians. And as the Greeks allowed the merchants to sell their wares on the common, the people, through Congress and the FCC, have granted broadcasters a franchise to operate in this forum. The American people did not give the airways away, and the private concessionaire has a responsibility to roll his carts and merchandise off the square when it is needed for serious public business."

I agree, and I believe it is therefore imperative that Congress pass legislation providing a minimum amount of program and spot-announcement time to candidates for the House and Senate and for President at 30 per cent of the regular commercial rate. Each would then be assured of a minimum chance to be seen and heard, and the electorate would be assured of an opportunity to make a more informed judgment on the candidates and the issues.

More basic, I hope the Congress will adopt changes in our tax laws which would permit a married couple

or single taxpayer to take a credit against taxes of one-
half of any contribution to a political candidate for any
office or to any political party, up to a contribution of
$50. The maximum tax credit allowable, then, would
be $25. Presidents John F. Kennedy and Lyndon B.
Johnson both vigorously supported the idea of public
financing or partial financing of campaigns, and in
late 1969, a tax-credit proposal in line with what I
have here suggested, cosponsored by Senator James
Pearson of Kansas and Senator Edward Kennedy of
Massachusetts, received forty-five votes in the United
States Senate and, thus, came very close to passage.

Public and Congressional support for this idea is
growing, and rightly so. It would encourage wider individual and voluntary financial participation in politics, leaving it to each taxpayer to decide to whom or
what party he would make his contribution, and would
result in greater confidence in public officials and in
the American political system.

President Nixon, disappointingly, vetoed the only
bill relating to campaign expenditures which the Congress was able to pass in 1970, a bill limiting the
amount of money each Congressional candidate could
spend on television. This action was most unfortunate,
but at least it served to demonstrate who was on what
side of the issue of popular control of the government.

Reform is also greatly needed in the present laws
relating to corrupt practices, limitations on political
contributions, and disclosure of campaign funds, but
of at least equal importance is the need to make sure

that a person can continue to run for public office in America without having to be wealthy himself or too dependent upon others who are wealthy and whose interests may not coincide with the public interest. We have rightly felt in this country that the general public is properly served by the granting of tax incentives for contributions to charity. Why would it not also be good public policy to give similar, although restricted, tax incentives to one who wants to contribute to the very workings of our system of self-government?

During the testimony of the late Senator Robert F. Kennedy before the Senate Finance Committee in favor of a tax credit for political contributions—after he had successfully opposed the proposal of Finance Committee Chairman Russell Long of Louisiana for a system by which a taxpayer could designate one dollar from his taxes to go to one of the political parties, a system Senator Kennedy properly thought would place too much power in the national parties—an amusing exchange took place among Chairman Long, Senator Kennedy, and Senator Albert Gore of Tennessee:

SENATOR KENNEDY: I would say for those individuals who do not file an income tax, they would have to go along and continue as they are at the present moment. But for all of the others who do file income tax returns, this would be a tremendous incentive to make contributions and participate actively in a political campaign.

The advantage of this plan, Mr. Chairman, is that

it would be not just for the presidential campaign, not just after the nominations have taken place, but during the period of the primaries, which is so important.

You talk frequently about the little boy born in the manger, that you think should be elected President of the United States.

THE CHAIRMAN: I think he would be qualified.

SENATOR GORE: There was also one in the bulrushes.

SENATOR KENNEDY: Yes, someone in the bulrushes, and Frank O'Conner in New York. (Laughter)

THE CHAIRMAN: The one in the bulrushes did not make a bad leader, may I say, from the standpoint of the Judeo-Christian religion.

SENATOR KENNEDY: That touched me very deeply, so I thought if we could make it possible for a lot of people in the United States to make a contribution, it would be most worthwhile.

Senator Kennedy then closed on the more serious theme of his testimony, saying, "Parties and candidates to take advantage of a tax credit will have to contact millions of individual citizens—to persuade these individuals that the parties and candidates are worthy of their support. The parties will have to listen to these individuals; and they must inevitably draw closer to the American people themselves."

The elder Robert M. LaFollette was said to have been encouraged toward his vigorous public career against privilege by the words of Wisconsin Chief Justice Edward G. Ryan, who declared in 1879, "The question will arise, and arise in your day, though perhaps not fully in mine, 'which shall rule—wealth or man; which shall lead—money or intellect; who shall fill public stations—educated and patriotic freemen, or the feudal serfs of corporate capital?' "

That is the question we must continue to ask. And we must act so that the answer to that question will continue to be in the people's favor.

CHAPTER VII

THE BULLY PULPIT

Afight with an incumbent President of the United States can be an uneven struggle.

Presidents only *announce* their decisions in public. As a rule, except where internal disagreement may be ferreted out by the press, they *make* their decisions in private. Thus, those who watch Presidents see a tidier image than those who look at the necessarily several-headed party out of the White House or the operations of the Congress. These latter make their decisions out in the open with a maximum of public bickering and time-consuming, often confusing debate.

It is generally easier for a President, then, to win adherents to his position from among the general pub-

lic than it is for the opposing party, all other things
being equal. His team seems to give extra reason for
confidence in its views because its members usually
appear harmonious and mutually reinforcing, while
the members of the other team seem always to be
elbowing their own teammates away from the goal.

There is quite a little of the monarchist left in each
of us. That part of us had just about as soon have a
neat announcement of what is right than be bothered
with all the process of winnowing out arguments and
arriving at a decision, a process which bothers and
worries us because it involves us.

And democracy, which is exemplified best by legislative bodies rather than by executives, *is* indeed a
clumsy and awkward process which often makes a spec-
tacle of itself. "He who would retain his respect for law
and sausages," Bismarck said, "should never see either
being made." Think, also, of the other advantages the
office of the Presidency has in the public attention it
gets and in the ability it has to build up and benefit
from patriotic fervor.

It is a true and powerful statement that "We only
have one President at a time," and "Hail to the Chief"
is his song. No other public figure in or out of office
can so stir up and focus the patriotism which runs
deep in Americans.

And no other office can command public attention
to the degree the President can. He speaks from what
Theodore Roosevelt called a "bully pulpit." Newspapers front-page his most casual dicta, and any net-

work television show will be pre-empted by him if he asks it.

The great political *disadvantage* of being President is that, at least for the long pull, one is judged by the results his policies produce; good intentions will generally not suffice.

This may not always be fair. The late John Collier, for example, while serving some years ago as Commissioner of Indian Affairs, appeared before the Navajo Indian Tribe at a mass protest meeting against government policies. Member after member of the tribe arose to state in strong and emotional terms his specific grievances against the Commissioner and the government. Among other programs inaugurated during his term, Collier had instituted an intensive tuberculosis-testing project which had discovered a very high incidence of the disease among the Navajos, and when those in the protest meeting had finally seemed to run out of additional complaints to voice, one Navajo man in the back of the meeting arose to say, "And I'll tell you another thing, Commissioner: we didn't use to have TB on this reservation, either, until you came into office!"

Presidents are accountable for what happens during their term in office. This accountability is what makes the American system work. By and large, the American people will not accept excuses, and this serves to offset somewhat the enormous political advantages and powers of the Presidency. It also tends to force Presidents to act, and to act responsibly.

It was once said to be an axiom of Southern politics that a man could get elected by running against "the interests" and thereafter stay in office by quietly throwing in with the interests and publicly running against the "niggers and the Yankees." A variation practiced in my part of the country when I was growing up was summed up in the advice an old-time politician gave me when I first filed for public office. "Never run against your opponent," he said. "Run against somebody else you are sure most of the people don't like." /H 3 8 2 7

"When I'm running," he went on, "I always figure out who is the least liked person backing my opponent in each town in my district; then, when I go into that town campaigning, if it's the local editor, I set up my speaking right out in front of his newspaper office. I draw me a crowd, shouting, 'Gather around, folks, and I'm going to tell you how editor so-and-so and the political bosses got my opponent in this race against me because I'm for the people.' At the right time, I always challenge the editor to come outside and debate me before the crowd and answer my charges. Whether he does or not, I've got my opponent where I want him."

As old as this tactic is, it has by no means passed totally from use. To counter the effect of accountability, Presidents are not always above attacking straw men or supposed villains.

The Congress is a ready target. By late 1969, as President Nixon's first year was drawing to a close, it had already become apparent, for example, that two aspects of the economic policies of the Nixon Administration were beginning to cause serious problems.

For one thing, true both to his basic political philosophy and his loyalty to principal supporters, Mr. Nixon had announced and followed a hands-off policy in regard to price and wage decisions, even in the basic industries. He had said that his office would not interfere, that he would not engage in what had come to be called "jawboning"—that is, using the moral suasion and other considerable influences of the Presidency to hold price and wage increases within some reasonable voluntary guidelines. The use of the powers of the Presidency in this way, which had actually started during the administration of President Dwight Eisenhower, had become a major target of attack in some quarters, stirring up memories of President John Kennedy's public row with Roger Blough of U.S. Steel ("My father always told me they were sonsabitches," he was reported to have said about big businessmen) and President Lyndon Johnson's celebrated arm-twisting techniques. Strengthened in his natural inclinations by the opinion of his economic advisers that the guidelines instituted by previous administrations had been ineffective, President Nixon abdicated any responsibility in regard to private decisions to raise prices or wages except as those decisions might be influenced indirectly by the monetary and fiscal policies of the government. And he steadfastly kept to this position even when Arthur Okun, former chairman of the Council of Economic Advisers, clearly demonstrated that, while not perfect, voluntary guidelines backed by the White House had markedly helped to hold down wage and price increases during previous administrations and that the rate of increase had taken a demonstrable jump upward after the Nixon Administration abandoned guidelines. Steel and copper prices had gone up several times, and these basic price increases had rolled through the rest of the economy like ocean waves.

For another thing, again true to traditional Republican policy and his big bank backers, President Nixon had favored tight money and high interest rates as a means of slowing down and cooling off the economy. While economists were in some disagreement on precise details, by the end of 1969 most of them were in agreement that the tight-money, high-interest-rate policy had been too severe and in effect too long, and that there was a real danger of too great a slowdown in the economy and too much unemployment, if not an actual recession, which some accurately predicted.

In short, by the end of 1969, following a year of purposeful action and inaction by President Nixon on the economic front, big bank profits were the fattest in history, inflation was at its worst since 1951, unemployment was also continuing upward, and interest rates were at their highest level since the Civil War. Thus, in December 1969, one day before the next public announcement was to be made of the Consumer Price Index which would show another sharp increase in prices, President Nixon figuratively set up his sound truck in front of the office of the Congress and the Democrats and asked the people to gather around and hear how these groups were opposing him in his fight against inflation. It was a tactic later to be used by him again and again.

While I do not say it happened, one could easily imagine a scenario of how it all might have been set up: The curtain rises on a meeting in a room in the west wing of the White House. In the room, under the Democrats called "the Fish Room" and used for picture taking, now called "the Theodore Roosevelt Room" and used for "photographic opportunities," are gathered Presidential staffers Erlichman, Haldeman, and Dent. They are huddled around some papers which Erlichman is holding.

ERLICHMAN: (*banging the table with his fist*): It's going to be hell to pay. Here are the figures of the consumer price index which comes out tomorrow. Despite all our optimistic talk about "light at the end of the tunnel" and "right around the corner," read the words yourself: "the steepest jump in consumer prices since June." What's a poor President of the United States to do?

DENT: Who needs such reports? Let's not put it out!

ALL: Yes, let's not!

ERLICHMAN: I've already tried that, and it won't work. Arthur Burns says these reports have always been made for some reason or another, and they would be missed, even if we say they've been cut out to save money, which I suggested.

HALDEMAN: Let me run this up the flagpole, politics-wise: suppose the President pointed out that this is like the substitute center fielder who said that the last guy had messed up the position so badly that nobody could play it.

DENT: Well, that's good, all right, and we should use it, but we need something else, too, because a big thing in the election was our saying that President Nixon could and would get inflation under control.

ERLICHMAN: Yes, and have you seen the latest Louis Harris poll, which shows that the President gets a strong negative rating on his handling of the economy —worse than the negative rating we got in August?

DENT: Don't say Louis Harris to me! We ought to turn Agnew loose on him for a while, and we'd slow him down like we did some of those left-wing television commentators. Everybody knows he used to work for those Kennedys.

HALDEMAN: No, Erlichman is right, and other polls show it. We need something more. Saying the Democrats were no better—and, don't get me wrong, I'm all for it—is not enough. We need something more dramatic. Now, what would McLuhan do?

ERLICHMAN (*jumping up*): Eureka! That's it! We've got to *do* something, not just *say* something. That something must dramatize the President struggling against a villain on behalf of the people. Then, when

higher prices are announced tomorrow, that announcement will actually be a plus in our favor, because the
blame will fall on those we're fighting.

HALDEMAN: Well, the obvious villain is the Congress. Everybody knows they are spendthrifts.

DENT: Yes, but they've actually cut five-point-six
billion from the President's budget.

HALDEMAN: Then we've got to pick out some individual bill and veto *it* as spendthrift. The Congress is
the villain and the veto is the dramatic act. We can
announce it today, and that will take the play; to the
degree the consumer price index is noticed, it will
just reinforce the image of how hard our courageous
fight is against the forces of evil. But what bill can we
pick to veto?

DENT (*shouting*): Foreign aid! There aren't any
voters for that.

HALDEMAN: No, the Congress has already cut what
the President recommended for foreign aid by more
than one billion dollars. What about the Defense appropriations or something like that we can call "unnecessary expenditures"?

DENT: Absolutely not! The Congress has already cut
five-point-nine billion from the Defense budget which
President Nixon asked for, and our good friends like
Strom Thurmond can stand only so much. And don't
tell me you've got your eye on the ABM or the SST or
Space?

ERLICHMAN: No, Dent is right; it's got to be something else. What could we say we're going to veto that would automatically get a knee-jerk reaction out of the liberal Democrats in Congress and thereby dramatize that they are opposed to the President's fight against inflation?

HALDEMAN: I've got it! What's the worst word in the political dictionary? Welfare, of course! What federal department is hated most by the South and Sunshine states, as Kevin Phillips would put it? Of course, it is the Department of Health, Education and Welfare, with all their civil rights guidelines and liberal thinking! And the appropriation by the Congress for that Department is one-point-three billion over the budget right now.

DENT: Oh, how those Democrats will scream! I love it! But do you think the public will notice that, even with the increase for HEW, the over-all budget requests of the President were cut by five-point-six billion or that our threatened veto will result in less funds for such popular causes as cancer and heart research?

HALDEMAN (*putting an arm around Dent's shoulders soothingly*): The threat of the veto will be the main thing, and that's what will get the play. We can always compromise on things like cancer and heart research. But the people will get the message that the President is for holding the line on expenditures and the Congress isn't.

ALL: Then, it's decided. Let us go and tell the Chief.

HALDEMAN: Wait, remember the rule: if you *do* a

liberal or conservative thing, always *say* it's at least in part for the opposite reasons. We're doing a conservative thing. What's a liberal reason?

ERLICHMAN: Easy. Impact aid to schools is opposed by the more vocal liberals. Let's have Finch attack it a few days after the President announces his intent to veto the HEW bill.

DENT: Wait a minute! A lot of our friends will holler if we go against impact aid.

HALDEMAN: Don't worry. Once we establish our public image on the central issue of inflation and spending, we can have Hugh Scott and Gerald Ford pass the word that we will agree to restore all or most of the impact aid funds.

ALL (*joining hands and dancing around the table, singing*): "This is the way we make our laws, make our laws, make our laws. This is the way we make our laws, so early in the morning!" CURTAIN.

The meeting and the dialogue are fanciful, but the basic facts are not. A day before the December 1969 consumer price index was to come out, President Nixon announced that he would veto the HEW appropriation bill, even though it was over his budget by about the same amount the Congress had cut his request for foreign aid, even though the Congress had cut his request for Defense expenditures by $5.9 billion, even though he had asked for funds for the Safeguard Anti-Ballistic Missile system and for the Supersonic Transport plane and even though the total appropriations approved by Congress were still $5.6 billion under his total budget requests. The Secretary of Health, Education and Welfare, Robert Finch, criticized the impact aid program by which the federal government provides special funds to certain school districts for children whose parents live or work on federal military or other installations, while, later, the Administration acquiesced in keeping funds for this program largely intact.

Polls showed that the initial effect of the President's threatened veto of the HEW appropriation and then his actual and flamboyant signing of the veto message on nationwide television after Congress had refused to reduce the HEW funds (even though he later concurred in some increases over his budget for cancer and heart research and for impact aid funds) was to create a public impression that he was fighting mightily against inflation with no help from the Democratic Congress—indeed, that he was fighting inflation against their active opposition.

These Presidential tactics continued in 1970. The President went on television in June, more than one-third way through his term, to blame the Democrats and the Congress once more for the country's persistent economic woes, offering very little new action on his part. Soon thereafter he vetoed legislation to improve the Hill-Burton hospital construction program, and, late in 1970, an employment bill providing for hundreds of thousands of jobs and training slots.

The war in Vietnam was another issue concerning which domestic villains were very important to the

Administration. President Nixon, during the 1968 campaign for the Presidency, had promised to end the war, revealing no specific details of his supposed "plan" on the grounds that to do so would give aid to the enemy. A great many people obviously voted for him because he seemed the best bet to end the war and bring American boys home.

By late 1969, increasing numbers of Americans had become restive about the war. They wanted out, and they were worried about the fact that the Nixon policies seemed to be much like those followed by the preceding administration. A group of young Kennedy and McCarthy-type activists, led by Sam Brown and David Mixner and others, organized what was called a Moratorium on the war, to focus attention on the issues and to give voice to the growing opinion that the United States was not getting out fast enough.

In many ways, the evolution of my own views was parallel to the change in the way a majority of the general public probably came to regard the war. I was elected to the Senate in 1964, the year of Lyndon Johnson's overwhelming defeat of the jingoism and widened war policy embodied in the Goldwater campaign. I came to Washington from that section of America which, as well as any other, epitomizes the best aspects of patriotic love of country, and I came with all the preparation on world affairs and defense strategy which eight years in a state legislature affords one.

During my first years in the Senate, which postdated

the debate on the Tonkin Gulf Resolution, members of Congress were assembled down at the White House from time to time to hear reports on the war. These briefings featured the Secretary of Defense, the Secretary of State, the Director of the Central Intelligence Agency, the Chairman of the Joint Chiefs of Staff, and the President of the United States. We looked at charts which showed the "body count" of the enemy killed during the last week and the number of weapons captured. We heard how the number of desertions from "our side" had declined and how the "pacification" program was going forward with better-than-expected success. Everything was quantified, and, since it was quantified and certified by the highest authority in the government, it all seemed very logical and real. We were winning. Since we seemed to be winning, it was much easier to believe what we were doing should be done.

True, even then, a few "nervous Nellies" in the government—as well as a few people outside the government—were expressing doubts about the war, not only about its goals, but also about how it was going.

At first, the issues seemed simple: America against aggression; once the flag is there, we have to back it; if we don't fight there, it will be closer to home next; if we cut and run, no one will trust our word. But, little by little, doubts began to creep in.

My own change of position concerning the war came about finally in the spring of 1968. Senator Robert F. Kennedy got me and others together at a small private luncheon with Roger Hilsman, former Assistant Secretary of State, who had just come back from South Vietnam and Paris. Hilsman, an expert in counterinsurgency, had become convinced, among other things, that the continued bombing by us of North Vietnam was not only ineffectual but actually helped the North in rallying its own people and in influencing world opinion in its favor. He caused me to rethink my own position, and I became convinced that he was right.

Senator Kennedy, whom I admired greatly, had called me over to his house one night to read and comment on his first major speech disagreeing with the Johnson Administration on the war. He had felt that he was under special restraints in regard to the war because it would be said, whatever his motives, that he was breaking with the Johnson war policy for political reasons and that his own brother had followed the course from which he was about to depart.

"I agree with two-thirds of the speech, and I agree that you must make it," I had said to Senator Kennedy as he and Ethel and my wife, LaDonna, and I had shared a warm fire in his front room with his oversized dog, Brumis. "I don't agree that we should stop the bombing unconditionally, but I believe that your advocacy of de-escalation and the terribly persuasive way in which it is said will rank with President Kennedy's inaugural address." I wanted to believe that we were doing the right thing and that we were on the right track, that our course would ultimately be successful if we would only persevere. The luncheon with Mr. Hilsman thereafter tipped the balance for me.

After Senator Walter F. Mondale of Minnesota, one of the most promising new voices in America, and I had agreed to co-chair Vice-President Humphrey's campaign for the Presidency—because we liked him and we felt he had the best chance to win and to persuade a majority of the Congress to implement what we felt urgently needed to be done on so many issues —we pressured for a peace statement and for a separation from the Johnson position on the war.

In July 1968, prior to the August Democratic Convention, Senator Mondale and I met with Vice-President Humphrey in his Capitol Building office, off the Senate floor, to hear a reading by Mr. Humphrey of part of a speech on Vietnam which we understood had been largely written for him by a group headed by former Ambassador to Japan Edwin Reischauer.

Senator Mondale and I felt the speech had a good chance, if implemented as policy, of starting us on a de-escalation track toward a negotiated settlement and toward bringing American troops home. "Don't change a word," we told Mr. Humphrey that day.

Senator Mondale asked if the Vice-President had to clear the speech with the President. The Vice-President said that he did not intend to do so, but he did intend to tell the President he was going to make a speech of that general import when he saw him at a White House dinner that very night.

Days passed and the speech was not made. Administration spokesmen, soon after the dinner, began publicly to shoot down the idea of a bombing halt, without any allusion to the Vice-President, saying that increased enemy infiltration from the North made bombing-halt suggestions foolhardy and dangerous to the lives of American troops. The President, it seemed, had indirectly if not directly made any such statement by his Vice-President that might be aimed toward winding down the war appear to be impractical, if not unpatriotic.

I had word from Ambassador Averell Harriman, the head of our negotiation team in Paris, as well as others, that a hot debate was raging within the Johnson Administration on the question of a halt in bombing the North. Accordingly, I decided that I must publicly speak out as a citizen and as a member of the Senate to help influence the decision. Therefore in early August I publicly called for, among other things, an unconditional halt in the bombing to change the course of what I had come to see as an unjustifiable and unwinnable war. What I said received less attention in the United States than it did in Paris, where there was questioning of whether, since I was Vice-President Humphrey's co-chairman, my statement represented a trial balloon for a major shift in Administration policy. Unfortunately, it did not.

At the Democratic Convention in Chicago, my duties included liaison with those who were to help draft the platform. After conversations with the President of the

United Auto Workers, the late Walter Reuther, former Berkeley President Clark Kerr, and others, a Vietnam plank was produced, drafted principally by Washington Attorney David Ginsberg, which called for an unconditional bombing halt. In unmistakable, peaceful tones it employed the suggestions and much of the actual language Senator Edward Kennedy of Massachusetts had used in a recent speech suggesting what the United States should do to get out of the war. We met with the Chairman of the Platform Committee, Representative Hale Boggs of Louisiana, and notified as many people as we could within the Johnson Administration. Chairman Boggs agreed to support the drafted statement in the Platform Committee and asked us to lobby for it among members of his committee and with those who could influence the committee.

Thereafter, David Ginsberg and I walked the language around the Convention city. Choosing first to try to dampen opposition from the hawks, we saw Governor John Connally of Texas. "I don't particularly like it; I wouldn't have written it that way, but I suppose I could live with it if I had to," he said. We thought it would be good from our standpoint if he said exactly that. Then we went to Governor Robert McNair of South Carolina, Governor Buford Ellington of Tennessee, Governor John McKeithen of Louisiana, and others. Efforts were also launched to secure support from the Kennedy-McGovern and McCarthy forces.

At four o'clock in the morning of the day of the last meeting of the Platform Committee, David Ginsberg and Bill Welsh, a principal Humphrey staff member, came to my hotel room to tell me that aides of President Johnson had moved in and were opposing the Vietnam plank which had been so carefully drafted and for which support had been so painstakingly built. "What shall we do?" they asked. "Hale Boggs is threatening to resign if the President and Vice-President can't agree," they said.

I gave it as my strong opinion that it was time for a little moxie. "The Vice-President should say to those who are purporting to speak for the President that he is going to release the text of the Vietnam plank which he has proposed and that he hopes it will be adopted; if it is turned down, he will have done the best he could," I said.

Soon, emissaries were back with a *compromise* Vietnam war plank which eventually was presented to a deeply divided Convention. I refused to support it and would not take part in the hastily organized speech-making in behalf of its adoption led by my good friends Representative James O'Hara of Michigan and Senator Edmund Muskie of Maine, who had not been involved in the earlier efforts.

It was in that same context that I later advocated, with all the moral force and political reasoning I could muster, a strong and forthright statement on peace in the nationally televised campaign speech Vice-President Humphrey was to make in Salt Lake City. "This is our third and last chance," I said as we all sat in a hotel room in the wee hours of the morning of the day the Vice-President was due to broadcast the speech. Vice-President Humphrey agreed with me that night —and again the next morning as the debate continued to rage within his retinue—and the speech, though it still was not as strong or as clear-cut as I wanted it to be, was made, a speech which brought in twice as much money as it cost to televise and which marked the first turn upward in an otherwise dismal campaign.

Upon taking office as Chairman of the Democratic National Committee in January 1969, I made clear that I felt the Party had to offer constructive alternatives to the policies of President Nixon and that it particularly had to speak out on "the great moral issues of our day: peace, race, and poverty." Thereafter, from time to time during the year, I expressed my growing concern about the way the Administration was handling the war, but my words had little impact.

I did not feel that the war should be a partisan issue in the sense that the Democrats should attempt to gain political advantage from it. I did feel that the Democratic Party had an obligation to help create the climate within which the President could do the right thing—that is, get us out of that war more rapidly and systematically—without being fearful of political attack from our side for doing so.

By October 1969 it was clear to me that the Administration policy was not going to get us out of Vietnam unless greater pressure was brought to bear. Earlier troop reductions, although commendable, had not changed my opinion, nor did those announced later.

I called together a group of Democratic Congressmen and Senators for lunch and put two questions to them: "What can each of us do as individuals that we are not now doing to help end this war faster? What, if anything, should be our response to the Vietnam Moratorium planned for October 15?" The feeling was that we should do nothing in a partisan way but that, by introducing resolutions, making speeches on college campuses and in our home states on October 15, and by calling on other citizens to join in the observance, we should do what we could to broaden public support for ending the war and withdrawing American troops on a quicker and more systematic basis and for realistic and determined efforts toward a negotiated settlement and toward greater progress in the South to assure a more democratic, popularly supported government there in keeping with our primary goal of self-determination for the people of South Vietnam.

The news of this meeting was more sensational than it might otherwise have been, because on that same day President Nixon held a press conference in which he said he would not be influenced by the Moratorium. There were outcries that I was trying to make the war a partisan issue, that I had aligned myself and the Democratic Party with "hippies, yippies, and traitors," and worse. Especially in my home state of Oklahoma, I was the subject of unusually bitter vilification and charges that I was encouraging, if not actually advocating, student riots and violence.

Administration sources began to warn that Marxists and anarchists were behind the Moratorium and that widespread violence was planned. Some of my best friends in Oklahoma begged me not to take part. There and nationally, groups organized flag-flying and other counter-demonstrations, the *Daily Oklahoman* headlining this activity PATRIOTISM VERSUS MORATORIUM.

On the morning of October 15, 1969, I spoke on Vietnam to an interfaith prayer breakfast in Oklahoma City. Later that morning I addressed some five thousand students at the University of Oklahoma and, during the afternoon, spoke to a like number at Oklahoma State University. It was the most moving, most satisfying, most inspirational day I had spent since becoming a member of the Senate. I learned that the same was true, according to the news, all around the country. Peaceful, solemn throngs of unprecedented thousands had gathered everywhere to witness for peace; it was said that there had never been anything like it.

I therefore shared the hopes of all those who had taken part in so memorable an event that President Nixon, since he had been moved by the impending October 15 activities to announce a major television address on Vietnam for November 3, would take advantage of the growing sentiment against the war and use that occasion to announce that he was not going to make it *his* war, but was going to disengage from it rapidly, fully, and finally. I dared hope that he would try to bind up the nation so deeply divided on that issue. I hoped especially, at the very least, that he would say to the young people, those whose lives were most affected by the war, but who were because of age largely powerless to influence policy, that he had listened and had understood and appreciated their anguished cries. I even hoped that the President and other high officials might have been caused to contemplate whether our foreign policy generally was sufficiently in line with our professed ideals.

The President chose instead to make "the kids" the villains and to question the patriotism of those who disagreed with him. He lashed out in uncompromising tones, calling upon the "silent majority" to stand up for him and with him and to intimidate the dissenters. It was a sad night.

The next days were sadder. The Vice-President and the Chairman of the Federal Communications Commission attempted, with some success, to scare the daylights out of the press and television. The Vice-President, the Attorney General, and others launched the most shameful, motive-challenging name-calling that had been heard in the land since the witchhunting days of the late Senator Joseph McCarthy. Obviously there were to be no more "bring us together" calls. It was not enough to silence the opposition; they were to be destroyed if possible.

It almost worked. The letters and telegrams poured

in, and television and press photographers recorded the happy scene of the President receiving them. The House of Representatives passed a favorable resolution, and the President came down to the Capitol in person to thank them for supporting his "plan for a just peace." Initial polls showed overwhelming support for the President's handling of the war. Columnists wrote that he had defused the Vietnam war issue and on domestic issues, too, had his critics on the run.

The fundamental problems, foreign and domestic, remained unsolved, the basic questions unanswered.

That judgment still stands today, yet the slow withdrawal of American troops is alarmingly accompanied by occasional massive American bombing raids, by an apparently steady widening and intensification of the war in Laos, Cambodia, and Thailand, and, sadly, by a substitution of Asian death and anguish for American, which is the human meaning of the policy of Vietnamization.

CHAPTER VIII

THE RIGHT TO HEALTH
AND LIFE

What is going to happen to me and my family if I get sick?

That is a basic question typical of those to which the people are entitled to better answers than they are now getting. They have more than just the right to an answer. They have a right to decent health. Good health is not a matter of charity, where one lives, nor of what family he was born into. It is a right.

In July 1969 President Nixon said of health: "We face a massive crisis in this area and unless action is taken both administratively and legislatively to meet that crisis within the next two years we will have a breakdown in our medical care system affecting millions of people throughout this country."

That such a "breakdown" is already occurring is plainly evident. The people are entitled to know whether we will meet it with words or with action.

The richest, most powerful nation in the world can take no pride in the fact that we rank twelfth or worse in infant mortality among industrial nations, while in 1960 we ranked sixth. That we rank eighteenth in the life expectancy of men and eleventh for women is a disgrace. In 1953 we had the second-lowest mortality rate in the world. Now we are sixteenth.

While these general statistics are bad enough, they are even worse for some of our people. The infant mortality rate for nonwhites is almost twice as high as for whites. Maternal deaths are three and one-half times higher. Nonwhite Americans can expect to live seven years less than white Americans.

One-third of the three hundred thousand people who annually die in this country from cancer could be saved if proper care were available. Six thousand Americans with kidney disorders need not die each year from this cause.

Rising costs are no less a problem than failures in the health delivery system. There has been a 35 per cent increase in physicans' fees in the last five years— an increase double the increase in the Consumer Price Index. During the same five-year period, the costs of hospitalization have increased over 82 per cent.

According to an Associated Press survey not long ago, at Boston Massachusetts General Hospital the average bill is $120 a day; in 1960 it was $36.50. At

Mount Sinai Hospital in Miami Beach the average daily bill has increased from $57 to $112 since 1960. For all hospitals in the United States the average daily bill is now $67.59. That national average will soon reach the level in New York City, Los Angeles, and Houston—$100 per day.

The Associated Press reported concerning a Philadelphia patient who has been hospitalized for fifty years that the costs to the patient for hospitalization for the last seven years equaled the costs for the entire first forty-three years. A woman in Oklahoma, not old enough for Medicare and not poor enough for Medicaid, recently wrote me about her illness that had cost her over $2500 in medical bills:

"This letter is written to you," she said, "not begging for charity, but it is written in desperation of being in a seemingly hopeless situation. If, however, you have some suggestion as to what I can do, please let me know. But also please bear in mind that there seems to be this gap in the Medicare Program which leaves some people stranded and perhaps future amendments and legislation could be passed that would cover this type of situation."

It is an outrage that this woman who has worked hard all her life is left so utterly defenseless against such a common problem as ill health.

A Tulsa attorney who serves as trustee in bankruptcy in approximately one hundred fifty cases a year recently told me that illness and medical expenses are the cause of bankruptcy in the majority of cases with which he is involved.

"The typical bankrupt is between twenty and thirty years old," he said. "He has a wife. He has children. If he has been the one who incurred the illness the time at which he goes into bankruptcy is shortly after the illness occurs both because income stops and expense goes up. If it has been some other member of the family the time of bankruptcy is extended. It may be as short as six months; maybe five years. In that time he has devoted part of his income into payment of the medical bills and he has become indebted to any number of people in the community.

"Typically, when he became bankrupt he had a good job; his income may have been $600 or $700 per month, even. Maybe he did not have as good a job. In either event, since he was relatively newly married, he owed on his furniture, his car, and his home. It took virtually everything he had to meet the payments and there was no reasonable way by which economic planning would have permitted him to be in some other position.

"There were few, if any, government programs available to him because he was neither old enough to qualify nor poor enough to qualify."

There is something desperately wrong with a health-care delivery system which allows a young couple, just starting out together in life, to be wiped out by something over which they have so little control.

This country has a shortage of approximately 50,000 doctors. We rank seventh in the number of physicians per 100,000 population—behind Russia, Czechoslovakia, Bulgaria, Hungary, Austria, and West Germany.

Many rural areas and poor sections of urban centers face even more severe shortages of doctors. In Oklahoma it is not uncommon to find a rural county having only one doctor per two to three thousand persons. Two counties have no doctors. In some of the poorer areas in New York City the ratio is one to ten thousand.

Many doctors find it increasingly difficult to keep up with seeing some fifty patients a day. A rural doctor in Oklahoma recently told me, "We're tired; we're worn out. We work harder; we see our families disintegrate under these circumstances. We see patients day and night and are always interrupted by people's problems. We want you to know that we're working. If somebody wants to pay the bill and send people out there to help us, we'd be happy to have it."

But at a time when we need massively increased numbers of health personnel, medical schools are experiencing severe financial difficulties. In mid-1970, *Business Week* magazine reported that "43 out of the 107 [medical] schools in the U.S. are drawing federal 'distress' funds so they can at least last through the current year."

Dean James of Mount Sinai has said, "If the federal government has a long range, deliberate arrangement to cut medical schools by one-fifth they're on the right track."

Without drastic action, little hope exists for increasing the yearly output of graduates from our medical schools. In 1969 the figure was 8200, while the National Institute of Health says we should be producing doctors at a rate of 20,000 per year between now and 1980.

Shortages in numbers of other health personnel are equally acute. Already many hospitals and nursing homes find it difficult to meet federal standards because of the scarcity of trained people.

It is obvious that we must swiftly enact a comprehensive national health insurance program. Nothing else will do. It is not enough to allow the opportunity for good health to the rich, nor to provide it only for the poor and aged. The man in the middle is also entitled to protection.

All of our people are entitled to good health. This new system, patterned after or as a part of the Social Security system, should be based upon the insurance principle of prepayment but with a large portion of its costs also coming from government funds.

We know from the experience of other industrialized countries, whose health statistics are better than ours precisely because they have established some kind of health insurance system, that such a system will work. The health statistics of these countries clearly show that they are doing a far better job of caring for people than are we.

Health insurance alone will not solve our problems. Unless we substantially increase medical personnel, a new health insurance system could further disrupt our health-delivery system. Evidence clearly indicates now that by enormously increasing the demand for health care through enactment of the Medicare and Medicaid programs we caused a serious rupture in the system, because we did not at the same time provide for equally massive increases in supply. We did not provide, as we should have, for the simultaneous increase in health facilities and personnel to accommodate the greatly increased demand for health care which these new programs engendered and sought to serve.

The fact is that, as Congresswoman Martha Griffiths of Michigan has stated, we face "a sophisticated 20th century technology shackled to 19th century organizational patterns."

Therefore, we must encourage a reorganization of the health delivery system, providing incentives for group medical practice and comprehensive preventive care. We must also massively increase the numbers of subprofessional and paramedical personnel.

In short, we must increase the effectiveness of present manpower and also increase the number of available manpower.

In the late 1930s, industrialist Henry J. Kaiser, in order to provide proper medical care for his workers on the Colorado River project, set up a program for providing total medical care to these workers on a fixed fee, prepaid basis. That program was continued during World War II for Kaiser's workers and was later made available to the general public in California, Oregon, and Washington.

Under the Kaiser Plan, members pay premiums

which finance whatever medical care may be needed from the Kaiser Plan physicians, working together in group practice. The plan, now serving more than two million people, provides comprehensive care at an annual cost of $100 per member, two-thirds of the cost of comparable care throughout most of the country, according to Dr. Sydney Garfield, the plan's originator.

The Kaiser Plan has financed more than $267 million worth of facilities and equipment, and it funds some 2000 physicans and 13,000 nonphysician employees, as well as providing substantial amounts of money for teaching, training, and research.

Under the plan and similar ones in effect in New York, Detroit, and Washington, D.C., the patient can still choose his own doctor and the doctor has the free choice of patients. Every effort is made, as it should be, to see that the doctors involved have control over medical matters. There appears to be a growing indication on the part of younger doctors in the country of an increasing desire to have the kind of free time such group-practice arrangements permit.

"The collective experience of these plans has revealed some interesting facts," Fred Anderson recently wrote in the *New Republic*. "Our outmoded system typically requires four hospital beds for every 1,000 of population served; in the plans, half as many beds are enough because office visits and out-patient care are more intelligently used, and because there is no built-in incentive to over-utilize hospitals in order for the patient 'to get his money back' from insurance plans (which usually provide generous benefits for hospitalization but almost nothing for out-patient care)."

"The plans also keep drug costs down. For example, drugs for subscribers to the Seattle Plan cost fifty per cent less than the national average," Anderson stated.

While increasing the effectiveness of present medical personnel and facilities, through such means as incentives for group practice and preventive medical care, we must greatly expand funds for the training of additional medical and paramedical personnel through scholarships and loans and increased grants to medical and related schools. Hospital and other medical-facility construction must be funded at much higher levels.

Some 30,000 military veterans with training in health fields return to civilian life each year. Yet, because of low wage scales and lack of responsibility and prestige in the jobs they could presently secure in the field of medical care, most of them do not remain in health care jobs. Some beginning steps have been taken to capitalize on the skills these available numbers of men have, but much more can and must be done.

Group practice, comprehensive preventive care, and prepayment—coupled with a massive infusion of new funds to expand personnel and facilities—are the clearly indicated steps which must be taken with an unprecedented degree of urgency if we are to answer the anguished questions of millions of Americans, questions which arise out of present failures in our health-delivery system and alarmingly increasing medical costs.

In taking these steps, we must remember—as we most often have forgotten in the past—that our health-delivery system is supposed to serve the people and that, therefore, the people are entitled to a strong voice in the decisions which are made.

"The consumer must play a stronger part in establishing policy and making major decisions affecting the financing and delivery of health care," Mr. Walter J. McNerney, President of the Blue Cross Association, said recently. "The health professional left to his own prejudices tends to develop programs and institutions that are to a measurable degree self-serving. And in the last analysis important value judgments must be made beyond the limited point where the science of medicine is definitive. They are best made by consumers.

"This is not to imply that the health professional should not have a voice. He must. And he must have enough of an audience to guard against moves detrimental to the quality of care. But as between quality and effectiveness (both important), the second must prevail, and this is the realm of the consumer."

The right to health and life is fundamental to any statement of the people's politics. There are other basic questions to which the people are entitled to answers.

Where can I find work? What will become of me when I am old? What kind of life will my child have?

What sort of education will he receive? What will happen to me if I lose my job? Will my home and family be safe? Will America live in peace, so that I can pursue my own goals?

When politicians and political parties more forthrightly address these basic questions, which so dramatically touch the lives of the great mass of our people, the people will respond.

CHAPTER IX

THE DECADE OF
THE PEOPLE

★ ★ ★ ★

★ ★ ★

lack power to black people! Brown power to brown people! Red power to red people! Yellow power to yellow people! White power to white people!"

In Washington, D.C., the Howard University graduating class of 1970 was listening to a commencement address by that brilliant combination of black activist, Southern preacher, and exciting leader—the Reverend Jesse Jackson of Chicago. As he finished dramatically with the modern radical slogan "All power to the people," there were corresponding shouts of "Right on!" and everywhere throughout the audience clenched fists shot upward to match his own.

"All power to the people" is a radical slogan, but it

could also be taken as a shorthand restatement of the American governmental ideal of popular self-government, of government which "derives its just powers from the consent of the governed."

The great enthusiasm which the slogan evokes from various audiences throughout the country indicates that there is strong feeling in some quarters that the people are not sufficiently in charge. A great many Americans feel that frequently large, often bureaucratically complex, usually impersonal, and sometimes almost faceless corporations or labor unions or governmental agencies or educational and other institutions —and perhaps a combination of some or all of these at times—are making the real decisions which limit how they can live, restrict their future, and determine the quality of their lives.

There is truth in the Jewish adage "Pray for the government, for without it we would all devour each other." We have banded together to help each other. The weak must be protected from the strong. Organization and government will and must continue to exist.

Rightly fearful of untrammeled majorities, we have hemmed them in with certain limits on what they can do. Justly wary of concentrated power, we have divided and diffused it to guard against abuse.

We were not wrong in these basic assumptions, distrustful of too much power in one or many. But in carrying them out we also made the decision-making process in our government and society intricately complex, sometimes almost a labyrinth, difficult to master and negotiate with anything like immediate effect. In our time, in a huge and impersonal, highly mobile, urbanized, technological society with instantaneous communication and a greatly expanding population, our system's built-in resistance to any but gradual reaction has come smack up against the most radically different conditions and problems that could ever have been imagined. And the individual has tended more and more to get lost in the maze.

We are lucky that the genius of the American system is that it can accommodate at all to changed circumstances. We must now pledge rededicated allegiance to that genius, and we must speed up the process. We must either respond to this sense of powerlessness or risk being destroyed by it.

Decision-making needs to be decentralized. The individual must be taken more into account once again. The impersonality of authority has to be corrected. This is not an easy course. It is an ill-defined path with many confusing crossroads and wrong turns, and it is fraught with hazards and full of danger. It is, nevertheless, the way we must go, and the reward at the end is a society which more fully recognizes the value of every individual and affords him a greater degree of control over his own life, a goal worth the pursuit.

Every institution, public and private, must face up to the growing feeling of powerlessness which nearly all Americans feel—whether they are black or white, young or old, whether they live in the central city or the suburbs or the country.

"Money makes the mule go," we used to say in Oklahoma. Poor people lack the basic kind of power —economic power—which gives a person leverage in the modern world. Black people and American Indians and Chicanos and Puerto Ricans and others who are in some ways different from the majority of people in our society face special obstacles to the achievement of power and are now working on "getting it together" among their own people to confront the system with *group* power. Young people, who in this television era become aware at much earlier ages than ever before, are held out of "real" life longer than ever before because the same modern society which produced television also requires an ever higher level of skills and education from its participating members. Women, who are paid less for the same work and who do not have legal control over their own bodies, are rightly going to be heard from more and more. These are some who feel the sense of powerlessness most acutely.

But everyone in modern America feels it to some degree. What about the able-bodied worker laid off in an economic downturn? What about the mother of a sixth-grade child who cannot read? What about a secretary mugged between her office and her apartment? What about a father who finds that his son is on heroin and cannot find out which way to turn or whom to turn to? What about the old person whose retirement income is reduced by rising prices? What about the young couple who cannot buy a house because interest rates are too high and money too scarce? What about the businessman stuck in an elevator because of a power brownout, or the wife who cannot get her husband on the telephone because of the overloaded New York telephone system? What about the mother who knows her children suffer from chronic respiratory problems because of city smog? What about the oyster fisherman who sees his beds ruined by oil leaks? What about the conservationist who watches whole lakes and rivers killed by pollution? What about United States Senators who learn for the first time from a television broadcast that their country's armed forces have been ordered across an international boundary?

There is growing anger and frustration in our society with the way things are. The symptoms are obvious and many: narcotics in the suburbs, rising alcoholism, frightening crime levels, riots and looting by some and unconscionable shootings in the back by law-enforcement officials, student disorders and tragically unnecessary killings by National Guardsmen, beatings of students by construction workers while police seem to look away, burning or "trashing" of banks, ROTC and other buildings, and the shooting of Panthers in their beds.

The rhetoric is no better. Children are taught to say "pigs" and "honky." The Vice-President talks about "criminal misfits" and "radical liberals." Governor

Reagan says that if we must have a "bloodbath," so be it, and then says he did not mean it just the way it sounded.

It will not do to treat the symptoms. But neither can the causes be cured by more violence. A negotiated peace is desperately needed between man and society, today at war with each other, and a cease-fire is the first essential step.

We must formulate again for our generation and our nation the way in which we shall balance the demand for orderly processes with the right, even duty, of each individual to press for action based upon idealism and morality.

I cannot say here how the scale should be balanced in each specific case between the individual seeking freedom and the society which lives by consensus. But any technique of social change which destroys those aspects of society which allowed it to flourish is self-defeating.

In a society such as ours, violence is unacceptable first of all because it is inhumane and often hurts people. Too many people these days verbalize—and even fantasize—about violence as a tactic. Most of them would not think of taking part in it themselves.

"But there is already a lot of violence and cruelty here and in the world," it is argued. That is enough; let us try to end it, not add to it.

Zapata and the Mexican Revolution, an excellent book by Professor John Womack, Jr., of Harvard, details the depressing but true story of how the poor peasants of Morelos, under the honest indigenous leader, Emiliano Zapata, continually fought over many years against the powerful Mexican military, hacienda, and other interests to secure common justice, water rights, and agrarian reform. They sacrificed thousands of people in this process, seeing numerous members of their families shot as hostages and suffering untold hardships. But, for a long period of years, each time it seemed that victory had been won, it was only to witness the politicians take over and betray the revolution, compromise its goals, and sell out the interests of the common people for political power.

There is no question but that progress by many ordinary people was eventually made as a result of the revolution. There can be little doubt that, under the circumstances, revolution seemed the only avenue open. But two things about the Zapata experience stand out and have modern application. One, those who made the revolution spent vastly in terms of human life and suffering in the cause. Two, today, despite the revolution, Mexico is a one-party country where much human misery still abounds.

In the modern American context, where political-action alternatives are available and at hand, such an example should, it seems to me, serve as an absolute bar to advocacy of violence by anyone in furtherance of his personal goals, however just and in the public interest they are thought to be.

In other words, it seems to me—as lawyers would say—that the burden of proof is on the advocate of violence: to show that without doubt he knows what is best for other men in a given situation and to show without doubt that it is proper for some men to suffer and die for the goals he advocates. No one in America can sustain that burden and prove his case.

As one who thinks that it brutalizes human beings to kill or injure *animals* inhumanely, I am repelled by the rhetoric of violence and put off by those who would even flirt for a moment with the notion that bombings and maimings and killings of human beings for any American goal can be made to appear romantic or ennobling.

I come from a Western background where violence and force have been more enshrined in the folklore and everyday customs than anywhere else in our country. I can say with a certainty that men are more secure, less frightened, less subject to bullying, more able to be themselves and do as they please and follow their own inspirations today than they were even during my boyhood, when fist fights and gunnings were much more than a commonplace manner of deciding what was right or who was right in a particular case.

When strength is the test of right, weaker men must suffer spirit-killing ridicule and humiliation. The dude is an object of pity and the butt of the joke in the land of the fast draw.

Moreover, those who would not themselves take part in violent tactics are dishonest, I feel, if they romanticize about or in any manner appear to agree with such a course for others.

But, having said that, there should nevertheless be a clear understanding of the great urgency with which so many of the people of this country need reassurance that our system can and will respond fully to the pressing moral issues which call for action.

The depth of despair and hopelessness felt by so many of our brightest young people, for example, is frightening. It is exemplified by a letter I recently received from a young man who, as one in a group of about fifteen college students, had come home from school with my daughter, Kathryn, and had stayed at our house during the May rally and lobbying effort in Washington, following the invasion of Cambodia and the deaths at Kent State College in Ohio and Jackson State College in Mississippi.

The morning these young people prepared to leave our home to go to the mass rally in downtown Washington was the morning following the vicious attacks by construction workers on antiwar students in New York City, a frightening scene the young people staying in our home had watched on television the preceding night. Our guests were young, some only in their first year in college. They seemed, both the young men and the young women, thin and vulnerable—and they were scared. But, though most of them had not taken part in any large demonstration before, they— somehow, as young people of this era do—knew how to get ready. They each pocketed little plastic-encased supplies of Vaseline and put wet handkerchiefs in cellophane bags in their pockets—both to prepare against the possibility of encountering tear gas. They wrote my address and phone number on the backs of their hands with indelible ink—in case they were hurt or arrested and someone would need to call for help.

They desperately hoped there would be no violence. It certainly would not come from them; they were strongly opposed to violence. They wanted to be effective, and they fervently expressed their hope that the crowd would be large enough and orderly enough and impressive enough to have some effect on the President and the Congress. They were fearful as they left the house—but they left. They started off almost like soldiers, going to do their duty.

They came back from the rally early, before it was over, tired and sweaty, sunburned, a little put off by what one of them called "the tired old revolutionary rhetoric" they had heard so much of. Most wanted to do something more than rally or demonstrate.

They all wrote afterward, and the theme of what several said was very much like that of the boy who finished his letter to me by saying "I am still without a solution to the dilemma and would appreciate any advice that you might have, though I understand the difficulty of advising someone with whom you have such little contact."

The body of his letter explained the dilemma he felt

he faced, in a statement so typical of too many of our most gifted young people today:

This past year has been a difficult one for me and changes have taken place around me which are difficult to adjust to. My own politics have been becoming increasingly radical, buttressed by my own disillusioning experiences with the McCarthy and peace candidate movements.

In the end I have begun to believe that working within the system is just not a practical way to bring about the necessary change. That weekend of lobbying and rallying and especially my contact with Senator Blank Friday morning, though comparatively insignificant, was virtually the icing on the cake.

Yet, though I have rejected working within the system, I have yet to discover a viable alternative. SDS demonstrations and radical and/or militant action has appeared to me equally fruitless and increasingly ridiculous. I am left holding an extremely radical analysis without any means of acting upon it. The result has been that I have become increasingly cynical and quite unprepared to actually deal with the political situation in any real way. I find myself persuading people to take action that I, myself, will not take and doing things that I could never defend rationally or persuade another to do.

Both sides of the war issue have for too long used young people to do their work. Some have used them as political opponents, playing upon the terrible fears and hatreds which even peaceful student dissent stirs up in so many people. Others of us have not shouldered enough of the burden ourselves, have not worked hard enough and actively enough within the system to make it work and to make it more responsive and responsible.

Violence is not acceptable in our society today because it tends to undermine the very institutions of free speech, of assembly, of the right to petition our government peaceably, which are the provided means by which grievances can be heard and relieved. In a very practical sense, it often leads to active repression, not just of unlawful violence, but of lawful dissent as well. Violence is also unacceptable in modern America because it does not work.

Labor, it is declared by some, made historic gains toward realizing its rights through the use of violence. That is not true. A staff report for the National Commission on the Causes and Prevention of Violence, prepared by Hugh Davis Graham and Ted Robert Gurr in 1969, went into this matter in great detail. "There is no evidence that majorities will supinely accept violence by minorities," the study stated. "The fact that rioters are fighting for a just cause or reacting to oppression has not, in the case of labor, led to the condoning of violence by the public.

"The effect of labor violence was almost always harmful to the union. There is little evidence that violence succeeded in gaining advantages for strikers. Not only does the roll call of lost strikes confirm such a view, but the use of employer agents, disguised as union members or union officials for advocating violence within the union, testifies to the advantage such practices gave the employer."

Detailing how violence caused repression rather than progressive changes in labor laws and that progressive labor legislation came only many decades after labor violence, when public sentiment against labor violence had cooled and had changed, the study stated, "A community might be sympathetic to the demands of strikers, but as soon as violent confrontations took place, the possibility was high that interest would shift from concern for the acceptance of union demands to the stopping of the violence."

"The evidence against the effectiveness of violence as a means of gaining concessions by labor in the United States is too overwhelming to be a matter of dispute," the staff report to the National Commission on the Causes and Prevention of Violence concluded.

"But look at the blacks," some people say. "They would never have gotten so much attention without the riots of the summer of 1967!" The very people who say this are frequently the same people who are quickest to charge that the Kerner Commission, appointed to report on those riots, accomplished nothing and that, one year after its report, another study showed things one year worse.

The truth is that it is easier to infiltrate the PTA than it is to bomb it. It is cheaper in lives and property expended. It is more humane. And the result will most likely be more acceptable and more lasting. I do not believe it can be shown with much probability that revolutions are of an inherently continuing nature. Rather, it can be shown with more certainty that revolutionary governments are a little slow in withering away and that those who win their power by force are even more reluctant to share it or give it up.

The question is not necessarily whether people are inherently decent and good. But if one says they are, some of today's revolutionaries and anarchists will disagree with a torrent of angry and bitter words, which should make one wonder all the more, if they are right, why some inherently evil men, chosen by themselves, should be allowed to govern others, or why one should not expect the strong to prey with greater viciousness upon the weak if there were no state.

Indeed, it can be shown that anarchist activities lead not to less government but are more likely to lead to more government, more repression. If the choice is anarchy or repression, I have no doubt that that awful dilemma will be resolved on the side of repression.

Consider a recent CBS poll which reported, as had been found before, that most Americans, when not told they were being asked about the Bill of Rights, gave answers to specific questions which indicated their disapproval of those hard-earned safeguards in practice. Seventy-six per cent of those answering said that extremist organizations should not be permitted to organize demonstrations against the government, even if there appeared to be no clear danger of violence. Fifty-four per cent would not allow all individuals the right to criticize the government if such criticism was thought to be damaging to the national interest. Fifty-five per cent felt that newspapers, radio, and television, even though it was not in time of war, should not be allowed to report news the government felt was harmful to the national interest. There is a lot of fear in this country. And it is not all in the hearts of average citizens who are unskilled in the niceties of constitutional law.

Consider "preventive detention." One wonders who has the current concession on manufacturing euphemistic phrases to mask such ugly concepts. Congress has already passed for the District of Columbia what might be a pattern for the rest of the country. It is called "preventive detention" and grants the courts power to hold a person in jail without bail on the likelihood that he might commit a crime if turned loose on society, when the interests of society and the individual clearly would best be served by providing instead for a speedy trial and a decision on a specific charge.

There comes to mind a vague television image of the late Senator Robert F. Kennedy questioning a California grapeworker-country law-enforcement officer who said that it was the common practice to pick up and jail some Mexican-Americans on Fridays before they could get drunk and cause trouble, and of Senator Kennedy asking, with his incomparable mixture of incredulity and acid sharpness, "Have you never read the Constitution of the United States?"

Congress has also already approved what has been more descriptively termed the "no knock" proposal, whereby a law-enforcement official can obtain a court order which would permit him to break in a person's door without knocking if it is suspected that the house may hold narcotics that otherwise might be disposed of rapidly. "A man's home is his castle," it is said, and it is well known that a person may legally shoot one who without warning breaks into his house, if the occupant believes the intruder for unlawful purposes threatens the life of himself or his family. And that is just what some black leaders in the District of Columbia have publicly advocated if this proposal is used by the police.

Is this the kind of society we must become? I do not think so. The world was changing in the nineteenth century when Matthew Arnold wrote that he was "Wandering between two worlds, one dead, the other powerless to be born." While we, today, are at the center of an even mightier swirl of change, we need not accept Arnold's sense of helplessness. We can, instead, adopt the spirit of another eminent Victorian, Alfred, Lord Tennyson, expressed in a line the late Senator Kennedy claimed in part for the title of his last book: "Come my friend, 'tis not too late to seek a newer world."

Is there yet time for a change in the unhappy trends? Is there still an opportunity to restore America's self-confidence and rebuild its self-image? Is there yet a chance to restore the human trust which has been the glue that has bound us all together? I hope so, for if there is not, the questions will be academic and our lives and our society will be different in ways we will not like. Will it be easy? No, but as a good book title says it, *I Never Promised You a Rose Garden.* And we must try because there is no better alternative.

First, though, we must recognize the problem: awful, wrenching change which has made of our children what Margaret Mead has called "first generation natives" and has caused so many of the rest of us to suffer, as Alvin Toffler put it, from "Future Shock," bewildered and disoriented by change which has come and is coming more rapidly than we can assimilate it, leaving us with no role-models we can emulate or pattern our lives after.

Most Americans grew up at a time when depression and hard times either were realities or were strong and justified specters of the mind. Security tended to balance a little heavier in the scale of personal goals than did individual freedom and self-expression, material things a little weightier than idealism. "Success" in those terms has been attained by a majority of our people, but it has not necessarily brought happiness.

We must now balance the scales a little better, because we can now afford to do so, and because nothing else will work.

The 1970s can truly be the Decade of the People if we will move vigorously to do two things: return power to the people—open up our political parties, decentralize authority, broaden popular participation in political and other processes, and expand the people's control over governmental and other decisions; and if we will remember that there are no purely political choices, only moral ones.

When Martin Luther tacked up his ninety-five theses on the church door at Wittenberg, it has been said that he thereby sowed the seeds of our present troubles. No church or organization or national government can today claim or enforce pure faith in its entire teachings or unquestioning belief in all its dogmas. While it may make one more nearly a man, in the human sense, to arrive freely at right choices, not to know with a certainty what one must or should believe is most unsettling. It is the old but always intertwined combination of beatitude and pain. For the blessing of individual freedom of choice, we must suffer the anguish of self-doubt.

The statements of many college students come to mind. But it is not so much that such young people question the ideals of the rest of us as it is that they question whether we, ourselves, really believe in those ideals today, since our practice falls so far short of what we preach.

We are most troubled and our national troubles have grown worse because we have not fully acted on what we profess. We have compromised on right and wrong too long and too many times because we thought or were told that that was the only practical course. The truth is that, as the late Walter Reuther put it, "Idealism is the pragmatism of our times."

"Americans," wrote Peter Shraag, a World War II immigrant to this country, "have always been in some sense, out of place, living through the tensions between regional and national citizenship, between things accomplished and things undone, between promises extended—equality, justice, opportunity— and promises fulfilled. But through all this, belief in our national citizenship—its ideals, its mythology, its expectations—remained vital and alive. We were in tension with what we believed existed, not with what we suspected had ceased to be."

If women, poor people, blacks and other minorities, and young people are too aware today to settle for decisions in which their participation has been unjustly restricted or to accept expediency in place of idealism, so, perhaps to a lesser degree, are we all—and so should we be.

If we would only see it, the average worker or the "hard hat" is as upset about modern American life as is the young campus radical or the black militant. At least until the onset of recent economic policies, his hours and pay were rather good, his vacation, health, and other benefits fairly acceptable. But, he, like us all, needs to feel more important. He wants to be part of something larger. At the end of the day, once in a while he must ask himself, "What am I doing with my life? What am I really doing that is worthwhile? Where is the value in what I am and in what I do? Where is the worth in my society?" Neither he nor any of us may choose those exact words, but the questions, articulated plainly or not, are still there and they nag at each one of us.

In many ways this frustrated idealism may be worse for the "Middle American," as Joseph Kraft has called him. Compared with college students, for example, he may be less able to verbalize or communicate this feeling. He has fewer avenues to express it otherwise, and, having to spend most of his time making a living, he has less opportunity to do anything about it.

Though equally as intolerable as student violence, it is equally understandable when the Middle American physically lashes out with the same vehemence—but generally more muscle—exhibited by the student radicals, as he reacts against those who seem to be his adversaries. Those who speak foully of God and country and burn the flag or spit upon it raise his hottest anger because they question the last values which help to lift him above himself.

Is it not possible that both sides of this confrontation might be made to see, before it is too late, that each acts from similar motives? Is it not possible that the fundamental idealism which runs deep in our society might not be better harnessed and more nearly made the central theme of our national life?

Real equality is "the right of every man to participate according to his aptitudes and powers, in the common endeavor to promote each by way of the other, the future of the individual and the species," wrote the great twentieth-century Jesuit philosopher Pierre Teilhard de Chardin.

"Indeed," he asked, "is it not this need and legitimate demand to *participate* in the Human Affair (the need felt by every man to live co-extensively with Mankind) which, deeper than any desire for material gain, is today agitating those classes and races that have hitherto been left out of the game?"

All of us—but particularly politicians, political parties, and governments—must recognize the practicality of idealism. People must have a better chance to be a part of something worth believing in. Participation in the cause of human equality, justice, and opportunity—here at home and around the world—is the only key to our own salvation.

CHAPTER X

PEOPLE AND
NATIONAL PRIORITIES

There are some who think that modern student protests are merely today's equivalent of the panty raid; there are others who feel that campus unrest and dissatisfaction can be settled solely by university reforms.

Activist young people today, while viewing the university as a prime place to begin wider changes, see more clearly than any previous generation the grievances which have for centuries burdened us and our country.

They are justly questioning a society which has always kept black Americans subordinate to other Americans.

They are properly questioning the priorities of a

nation which spends $70 billion for defense and only $4 billion for education.

They are rightly puzzled by the paradox of a country which can spend $2 billion a month in Vietnam but not that amount in a whole year to banish hunger altogether from our national life.

They justifiably worry about a society in which a majority of parents can give their children television sets, cars, and trips abroad but in which no parent can guarantee that his child will breathe clean air or drink pure water or walk safe streets.

These basic and fundamental questions must be met. As we grow more firm and sophisticated in our ability to prevent and put down violence, we must also grow more determined that ours will be a truly just society.

Universities must change, but society must change as well. For a great many of our people, young and old, continued faith in the American system requires that we set up our priorities in such a way as to make it clear that idealism, based upon the innate value of human life, is our central theme.

At the same time, for those Middle Americans who have become equally alienated, we must do a better job of helping them to see that their just complaints about high taxes and high costs, an intolerable crime rate and too much violence, and inadequate education and restricted opportunity for their children is very much a part of the present misallocation of national priorities.

All of us must come to understand better than we have in the past that the resources available to government to meet the various demands made upon it are not unlimited, and that, even after the end of the war in Indochina, we will still have to make difficult decisions about the relative importance of various national needs.

In short, therefore, if we are to respond to the sense of frustrated idealism which so many people in America feel and provide some replacement or supplement for the religious and other beliefs which for some have been destroyed or damaged—something to believe in, to work for and be a part of—and if we are to respond to the feeling which is also strong in America that "I'm paying more taxes than I ought to have to pay, and, still, everything about the country and my own life is getting worse," we must put first things first.

Today, we live in a country which has the highest rate of unemployment, the highest rate of public dependency, and the highest rate of population growth of any industrial country in the world.

Today, we live in a country which has not yet decided to live with difference, where the black or Indian or Chicano child still starts the contest considerably behind the starting line. In this, the richest and most medically knowledgeable, most agriculturally productive country in the world, 25 million people still live in poverty, too many little children are still hungry, and people still die needlessly of bad health because they are poor. We live in a country where the schools

in areas in which poor people live are often almost
criminally ineffective, and, together with our society's
tolerance of bad health, bad housing, and bad nutrition, are systematically destroying children, a destruc-
tion we pay for not only in the terrible expense of
moral schizophrenia but also through the costs of crime
and prisons, remedial education and special training,
welfare and dependency, alcoholism and narcotics.

About fifty years ago there were 100 million Americans. There are more than 200 million now, and—even
with presently declining birth rates—there will be 300
million by the year 2000. If we are already killing
about 55,000 Americans each year on our highways,
what will it be like then?

If unclean water and dirty air and noise and pesti-
cides are problems now, what will it be like when our
population has increased by an additional 100 million?
What about the problems of crime, transportation and
urban congestion, housing, race tensions, recreation,
urban problems, and health?

If it is true now that a computer can do about what
a high school graduate formerly did and that a person
of mediocre skills and education is a surplus seller in
a buyer's market, what sort of additional stress on the
educational system can we expect when the number of
our people has increased by an additional one-third?

What sort of a world will it be in the year 2000 if
present trends continue and the world's present population of 3.3 billion is more than doubled between now
and then, the greatest part of such growth occurring in

those countries where most of the poor and hungry already live?

We must begin to think of freedom in new terms. "We are beginning to discover that the right of free citizens to move freely without hindrance can be made meaningless by the breakdown of mass transportation, and the right of free assembly can be negated by impassable city traffic, or, for that matter, by uncontrolled crime in the city streets," Massachusetts Institute of Technology President Howard Wesley Johnson has reported.

"We are beginning to suspect that free speech and free press might become irrelevant if we were slowly strangled by the air we breathe, or slowly poisoned by our drinking water. We are beginning to see that equal rights and equal job opportunity, when finally obtained by those long denied them, can be made meaningless by intolerable housing conditions or by ineffective educational systems.

"We are beginning to realize that if exploding populations create a world of starving humans almost standing on each other's shoulders, all concepts of freedom can become irrelevant and American prosperity could be infuriating and incendiary to billions deprived of either hope or future."

How did we get into the mess we are in? Our governmental system has been remarkably stable and workable. Our people have enjoyed an extremely high standard of living and an exceptional system of training and education. Our science and technology and our industrial capacity are a modern marvel.

Each of us has known people who seem always to suffer continuous troubles and miseries which often appear to be almost self-inflicted. "People make their own hell," it is often said. So may it be with nations.

Perhaps we were too reasonable. I recall that in 1964, when I first came to the U.S. Senate, the total defense appropriation was about $50 billion. By 1970 that figure had grown to more than $70 billion. During that time the Defense Department was operating under budgetary methods, devised by then Secretary of Defense Robert S. McNamara, called Planning Programming and Budgeting System—or PPBS. The thesis of the system was that budget decisions about weapons, strategies, and Defense Department appropriations could be made on a more rational basis than had theretofore been the case. Prior to the administration of Secretary McNamara, the budgetary process began when a decision was taken at the highest level in the government as to what total amount of money would be allocated to the Defense Department. This total amount was then rather arbitrarily divided by the Secretary among the various services. The Army, Navy, and Air Force thereafter made their plans and decided upon projected expenditures within the total spending ceiling assigned to them.

Secretary McNamara decided that this old budgetary process could be put on a more rational basis, that strategies, plans, and weapon systems could be costed out and decisions made about their cost-effectiveness, that relative merits of various kinds of expenditures could be assessed, and that the general result would be more logical and more easily explained to the President, the Congress, and the country.

I feel certain that Secretary McNamara and others believed that this system would also result in holding down nonessential military expenditures and the size of the defense budget generally. That did not prove to be the case. Rather, once this smoothly logical system of explaining defense-expenditure decisions was instituted, it became even more difficult to mount a successful argument against any military appropriation thus so strongly buttressed and impressively presented.

In regard to defense expenditures especially, there may be much to be said for feeling. One might say, "I feel it in my bones that $60 billion is about all we ought to spend this year for the military, in light of our other problems and our total resources," and he would not be wrong. Arbitrary limits on military spending—other than war expenditures—may be about as effective as anything else in holding them within some sensible limits. Primarily, however, our budgetary difficulties arise from the past judgment we have made that we will accept considerable risks in other aspects of our national and international life, but that we must strive for *zero* level military or defense risks.

Of all the countries in the world, ours should be one which, having decided that we desire popular government and civilian control of the military, would recognize that military people are just the same kind of fallible human beings as the rest of us, except that they wear uniforms. True, they deal with awesome problems, but who does not these days?

I recall some years ago, when, as a member of the Oklahoma State Senate, I was taken on a tour of a brand-new missile-defense system near Altus, Oklahoma. The group of which I was a member was conducted through the underground control center and heard the almost eerie explanation of how the firing of the missiles could take place only as a result of a simultaneous decision on the part of the Air Force and the President of the United States, implemented through a secret electronic mechanism.

We then went deep into one underground silo where the missile, surrounded by all sorts of extremely complicated wiring and tubing, stood like a tall building. We rode an elevator from the powerful rockets at the bottom to the bulbous red nuclear tip at the top.

Within one month after my guided tour, all those missiles and all that complicated wiring and tubing were sold for scrap. We still have the holes.

"Department of Defense officials have a number of special perquisites, all of which bear close scrutiny," Senator Edward M. Kennedy testified before the National Priorities Committee of the Democratic Policy Council. "For example, the Secretary of each cabinet department is assigned a limousine, as befits his status. One exception is the State Department—the senior agency—which gets two. But Defense gets ten. Cabinet departments are also assigned additional chauffer-driven cars for the use of sub-cabinet officials. Agriculture, Justice, Labor and HEW each get four such cars. Defense gets seventy-six. The Chief Justice of the Supreme Court has a car; the Associate Justices do not. The top three officials in the Senate and in the House have cars; the other Senators and Congressmen do not. The startling aspect of these figures is, of course, the special treatment accorded the Department of Defense."

The point is that, while judgment should not automatically be made against whatever the military recommends, their recommendations should be subject to the same kind of careful scrutiny and examination as is given to the poverty program, for example. Yet, until the 1969 session, the Congress was likely to spend as much as two weeks debating a $2 billion annual appropriation for the Office of Economic Opportunity and then pass a $70 billion military appropriation bill in as few as two days.

With some measure of truth, someone once said that the amount of time the Congress spends on an appropriation bill is in inverse proportion to the amount of money involved. It is much easier to understand an item which costs $100,000 than it is to understand one which costs $1 billion.

But in the 1969 session of the Congress, $5.9 billion was trimmed from President Nixon's recommended appropriations for defense with no damage to national

security. For the first time on the floor of the Senate
there were detailed discussions—some in secret—on
strategic plans and new weapons systems. There was
both secret and public debate of President Nixon's
recommended Safeguard Anti-Ballistic Missile system,
and new funds for ships, planes, and tanks had to be
justified in detail, or were cut. This trend should continue.

It is about time that all of us more clearly recognized
that military risks are not the only ones—perhaps not
even the most severe—our country faces.

What about the risks we take by continuing to
move, as the Kerner Commission found, "toward two
societies, one black, one white—separate and unequal"? A friend of mine recently said that he was dis-
heartened when an acquaintance of his with whom he
regularly rode back and forth into New York City each
day, a man who had been a strong supporter of civil
rights causes, said to him on the train not long ago,
"There is something in what Pat Moynihan says;
Negroes have made a great deal of progress, and I
believe we ought to let up on those issues for a while."

"What do you do, read *The Wall Street Journal*
every day as the train goes through Harlem?" my
friend had asked him. I am afraid too many of us do
that. We see *Julia* or Bill Cosby on television, and we
assume that blacks have achieved full equality, when
the truth is that, except for a few showcase examples
at the top and a greater number of employees in the
lower-pay jobs, the television industry and most of the

rest of the American economy is a long way from providing equality of opportunity.

My friend's commuting acquaintance wanted to make a great deal of the fact that there are now a good number of black airline stewardesses. "What does that mean? I can recall when all the porters on the trains were black, and now a good many of those jobs are gone," my friend responded.

The gap between average white income and average black income has not narrowed; it has widened. The truth is that more than 90 per cent of all black children still go to all-black schools, and that 90 per cent of all white children still go to all-white schools. Ask me how, under those circumstances, we are going to become one nation, where men and women have learned to trust each other and live together, and I will answer that I do not know.

In 1970, the Department of Defense spent $39 million for public relations—not to recruit for the military or for public information, but to promote the programs of the Department of Defense. That was eight times more than the $5 million which the Administration requested for the entire civil rights–enforcement operations of the Department of Justice. What are the risks of continuing to be a society in which open housing and equal employment opportunity and integrated education are so timidly pursued?

With the best medical schools and hospitals and the best-trained medical personnel, how did America ever let things get so much out of kilter in the field of health? If we continue to hold back on doing what must be done to expand the number of medical and paramedical personnel greatly, to increase research, and to institute a system of universal health insurance to make sense out of our presently hodgepodge health-delivery system, what will be the cost? Who will live and who will die? Whether conscious or unconscious of what we are doing, each of us will help make those decisions.

What risks are we bearing from failure to act to meet the worst housing crisis since World War II, a crisis worsened by the unconscionably high interest rates in effect under the Nixon Administration's monetary policies and by an exploding population which means that we must build a duplicate America within the next thirty years? What is the cost to a nation of millions of children continuing to grow up in squalid slums or hopeless rural poverty?

What are the risks to our national security if we continue our presently half-hearted efforts against crime? Seventy per cent of those released from prison come back; yet there is no real funding of prison reform or prison rehabilitation. The Eisenhower Commission on the causes and prevention of violence stated that "violent crime in the United States is a phenomenon of large cities . . . a fact of central importance"; yet federal funds for this purpose are channeled primarily to the states, and a major city such as Cleveland, for example, received only $40,000 in 1969 from the $1 million allotted to Ohio. Though in 1969, the crime rate went up another 11 per cent, robberies climbed 15 per cent, and armed holdups increased by 18 per cent, we still are not willing to spend enough for enough policemen or to train them properly or to pay starting patrolmen beginning salaries of at least $8000. Nor are we willing to provide additional personnel so that a policeman can stop using up most of his time on duties other than crime fighting—traffic, clerical work, and family relations services.

Where is the money to expand personnel so that the courts can reduce shameful backlogs of criminal cases and grant speedy trials without allowing great numbers of habitual offenders to roam the streets or requiring them to stay in jail without bail until their cases come to trial? What are the risks of continuing to refuse to provide sufficient funds to prevent juvenile delinquency, the fastest-growing type of crime? When are we really going to crack down hard enough on organized crime, the size of which is obvious to all and makes cynics of too many good citizens?

When are we going to eliminate poverty and the other intolerable conditions which are the basic causes and breeding grounds of crimes, as the Eisenhower Commission so plainly stated and fully documented?

What are the risks to our society of continued overcrowding in the cities or of continued deterioration of our environment?

What price should we put on the growing risks our society is taking, as Senator Harold Hughes of Iowa has put it, from being "willing to spend almost any amount of public money to punish the addict, but nothing more than a pittance to provide the medical and rehabilitative services he needs to kick the habit"?

These are the questions which our country must be called upon to face and answer. As Senator Edward Kennedy pointed out before the National Priorities Committee, the 1970 federal budget amounted to about $1000 for each American, $400 of which was allocated for defense—and only $4 was provided for fighting crime.

He called attention, too, to the fact that, while continuing B-52 flights from Guam to South Vietnam at a cost (including munitions and fuel) of $50,000 for each such flight, the Administration's 1971 budget request for improving the nation's drinking water was $400,000 *less* than spent for that purpose during the preceding year.

Obviously, our first priority must be to end the tragic war in Indochina. Only then will we be able to begin to meet the mounting risks involved in our failure to act on domestic needs.

In the meantime, there is much which must be done to turn things around. *Fortune* magazine, in a report which was carefully done and justified in detail, showed specifically how, by bringing home some of our 320,-000 troops and their 250,000 dependents now in Europe at an annual cost to us of more than $12 million and requiring that the NATO nations assume a little more of their own defense burden, by deferring a new bomber fleet in this missile age and by holding up production of the new main battle tank and delaying other such items, more than $15 billion could be cut from defense appropriations without jeopardizing national security.

There is no reason for us to approve further deployment of an untested antiballistic missile system, as recommended by President Nixon, at a cost of untold billions. Rather, we should press for consummation of a mutually enforceable agreement with the Soviet Union in regard to defensive as well as offensive strategic weapons and thus provide ourselves far more security at far less cost.

The housewife at the shopping center would like to buy a great deal more than her funds will allow. She must, however, choose between a new dress for herself or new shoes for her children, between paying fully for the week's groceries or taking in a movie. Nations must respect similar restrictions.

If we had unlimited resources, it might be satisfying to embark upon the building of a recommended space shuttle at a cost of billions of dollars, leading toward an eventual manned landing on Mars. A supersonic transport plane, the development of which costs hundreds of millions each year, proposes to get a few of us to England a little faster by 1978; that might be all right if we could afford it. We can no more justify these expenditures now than we can the continuation of unlimited subsidy payments to huge-scale farmers.

If we are going to pull ourselves back together, if we are to raise an idealistic standard to which all our people can pledge renewed allegiance, now is the time for hard choices. As Senator Edmund Muskie of Maine has stated, there is something inherently wrong with the Administration's 1971 budget which balances $275 million for the SST against $106 million for air pollution control, $3.4 billion for the space program against $1.4 billion for housing, and $7.3 billion for arms research and development against $1.4 billion for higher education.

It is imperative that the Congress continue the kind of reordering of priorities that it seems to have begun. But two new mechanisms, I believe, are needed if the fight on priorities is to be won over the long pull.

I believe that there is a fundamental defect in the way we approve federal budgets and appropriations. For one thing, the President always asks for money only one year at a time. Under the present system, he does not talk to the country and to the Congress about long-range plans and goals, what he hopes America will be like ten or fifteen years hence. And, in the Congress, the committee system, with its narrow, jealously guarded and quite independent subject jurisdictions, often presided over by chairmen whose power allows them to ignore majority will, hinders the Congress in comparing the importance of one expenditure to another. One Congressional observer has said that expecting the Space Committee to make some judgment about the relative merits of a recommended space expenditure in comparison to, say, housing or education or health is, since the Space Committee only considers matters within its own subject jurisdiction, like the man who, asked how his wife was, responded, "Compared to what?"

Senator Walter F. Mondale of Minnesota, with my co-sponsorship and that of others, advocates legislation which would create a Council of Social Advisers to the President and require an annual social accounting to the Congress and the country. As the present Council of Economic Advisors helps to establish national growth, employment, and other economic goals and reports annually on the progress being made toward them, a report which the Joint Economic Committee in the Congress considers each year in detail, the Council of Social Advisers would be the mechanism by which national social goals could be set and an annual social accounting rendered, subject to full debate and discussion of both the goals and the annual accounting by the appropriate Congressional committees.

This or some similar new apparatus is necessary. I have no doubt that the Congress would never have approved, as it has done in recent years, spending at anywhere near the $5- to $6-billion level for the space program if the initial request had been made to the Congress in vague terms of learning about space and space technology. But the specific goal of landing a man on the moon and bringing him safely back to earth by 1970 was a dramatic and specific goal which caught the imagination of the public and won the full support of the Congress. We must set similar goals for ourselves in mental health and in cancer research, in housing and in teaching our people to read, in saving the environment and in making the streets safe. Our whole country can and must be caught up in this new adventure, and all of our people must come to await with anxious expectation each regular announcement of measured advance.

I believe that we need, second, a new agency in the federal government, cutting across all departments and reporting directly to the President, whose job it will be to implement a basic Bill of Rights for all American children. The taxpayer who curses the unemployed father he believes to be a malingerer can, nevertheless, be made to understand that the real or supposed sins of the father should not be visited upon the child. I believe that Americans will support the idea that every child in this country has certain rights, which are not matters of charity, such as the right to enough to eat, the right to good health, and the right to a decent education.

Several years ago, while visiting a small village in Guatemala called Chichicastenango, my wife and I sat for some time in a public market which the Indians of that area had maintained there since long before Columbus, observing the commerce and the people. Accompanying us was a medical doctor serving with the local office of the U.S. Agency for International Development, Dr. D. W. MacCorquodale, an unusually perceptive and sensitive man. "See that young Indian girl whose hair is russet or light brown and whose stomach is distended?" He nodded toward an eleven-year-old walking by us, carrying produce. When we said we did, he told us that her bleached-out hair and the other symptoms indicated that she was suffering from an extreme case of malnutrition and protein deficiency.

Kwashiorkor was the name he gave to this pitiful condition. It was the first time I had heard the word. Some years later, I learned with dismay, as did the nation, that it existed here in America and was found in a black ghetto in New York, on Indian reservations, and among migrant workers in Florida.

Despite the fact that, as experts such as Dr. Charles Lowe, Chairman of the Committee on Nutrition of the American Academy of Pediatrics, have stated, that "In effect the quality and quantity of nutrition given during the first formative years of life may have the effect of programming the individual for all the years of his life," the Nixon Administration's 1971 budget request sought less than half the money necessary to provide free lunches for poor school children and less than one-third enough to finance an expanded food stamp program the Senate had approved.

I believe that new national priorities and goals, expressed in terms of children and their rights, could inspire widespread public support and that the majority of the people of our country could be led to join in such an historic quest in a way that would lift our national spirit as nothing else could do.

One isolated aspect of human needs today in America—the health of American Indians—provides a stark example of the shameful injustices our present priorities produce and condone. If America generally faces a well-documented health crisis, consider how much more acute that crisis is for American Indians, Eskimos, and Aleuts.

Most Americans have begun to recognize the injustices endured by American Indians in the past. But more and more Americans must also begin to realize that injustices and broken promises are still suffered by American Indians—that present and past injustices have produced terribly damaging and lingering impact.

The level of health of American Indians, Eskimos, and Aleuts lags twenty to twenty-five years behind the health advances of the general population in America —and we have seen that this itself is highly unsatisfactory. The average age of death for American Indians is forty-four years, about one-third less than the national average of sixty-four. American Indians are eight times as likely to suffer from tuberculosis as the rest of us, and deaths due to influenza and pneumonia are nearly two and one-half times higher for American Indians than for others.

If one is an American Indian, he is ten times more likely to suffer from rheumatic fever, strep throat, and hepatitis. The incidence of otitis media, a middle-ear disease which leaves hearing impaired, is far more prevalent among American Indians than among any other people in our society.

Twenty-eight per cent of all Indian homes still lack running water and an adequate means of waste disposal. The average American Indian family of five or six members still lives in a one- or two-room house, and only about 24 per cent of the dental-care needs of American Indians are being met.

Amoebic and bacillary dysentery is thirty-five times worse among American Indians, and the death rate for American Indian infants between the ages of one and eleven months is three times that of the same age group in the general population.

Because of personnel shortages, it is not uncommon for one nurse in an Indian hospital to be responsible for more than one floor. Members of a patient's family, untrained in medical care, often have to be called upon to assist.

Physicians in Indian hospitals frequently have an impossible patient load, and physicians working in field stations or clinics see as many as eighty patients a day. One physician at an Indian hospital in Oklahoma in 1970 had a patient load which allowed him only three minutes per patient per day. The result of this type of overloading is long lines and degrading treatment.

The Indian Health Service has stated that outpatient visits during 1968 and 1969 increased 6 to 7 per cent a year, but there was no provision for a corresponding staff increase. In fact, after expenditure controls were implemented in 1968, there was an actual decrease in personnel working in the Indian Health Service—218 vital positions in the hospital health activity of the Service were lost.

In order to meet the staffing requirements for Indian hospital facilities, 225 to 250 employees are needed for each 100 average daily patients hospitalized, and 120 employees are required for each 100,000 outpatient visits. In fact, however, in 1968 the Indian Health Service was staffed with only 165 employees for each 100 average daily patients and with only 47.8 employees for each 100,000 outpatient visits.

Along with shortages of personnel, most of the Indian hospitals have serious drug shortages. In 1970, an Indian hospital in Oklahoma chosen at random was telephoned by my office to determine its needs for drugs and supplies.

The administrator of the hospital reported: "We have in the past run out of essential antibiotics—penicillin, ampicillin injectible, tranquilizers such as the antidepressant librium, and analgesics (pain relievers), as well as Darvon and aspirin on occasions. At the present time we are completely out of Florinal—dentists use this for pain from extractions.

"Essidrix, which is a diuretic most essential for removal of fluid from the body, is often not in stock. From time to time, we have run out of birth control pills.

"At the present time there are no baby vitamin drops and we have not had any for at least one month. On occasion we have run out of cough syrup. Also, a very inexpensive item, sodium salicylate, used for rheumatoid arthritis, is often out of stock, as well as Indocin, which is a more expensive drug used for rheumatoid arthritis.

"The hospital stockroom would need $18,000 in order to bring their stock up to a safety stock. These items are surgical items such as sutures, examination gowns, gloves, X-ray film, Band-aids, bandages, paper towels, and other items. In the past we have had to give diabetics reusable syringes because we did not have disposable syringes.

"Our basic problem is that we cannot obtain sufficient supplies so as not to run out before we can get funds to replenish the supply.

"At present we have a shortage of approximately twenty-one people in the hospital, and the lack of help has required a lot of unpaid overtime on the part of the whole staff in order to care for the sick."

Earlier reports from other hospitals in Oklahoma indicated that testing for tuberculosis had from time to time been discontinued because necessary supplies were not available, and that in 1969 influenza shots could not be given to more than 600 Indian students at Chilocco Indian School because the vaccine was not available. Almost all of the hospitals reported that they were sometimes either low in supply or out of many of the most basic and most needed drugs.

With the tremendous increase in medical costs, increases in the Indian Health Service appropriations have not really resulted in increases in the level of care. In 1968 the appropriation was $84,862,000; in 1969 the appropriation was $91,710,000; in 1970 the appropriation was $101,529,000; and for 1971 the budget request was $113,217,000. This is a percentage increase from 1968 to 1971 of approximately 33 per cent, yet the cost of providing the same level of medical care by the Indian Health Service during the same period has increased approximately 34 per cent.

There is little hope that any significant changes will occur in the shameful statistics regarding Indian health or that the shocking lack of personnel and drugs in Indian hospitals will materially improve unless there is a substantial increase in funds.

As the Indian members of the National Council on Indian Opportunity stated February 16, 1970, "In light of the dire need for all health facilities and health needs, it is criminal to impose a personnel and budget freeze on Indian health programs. Even without a freeze, Indian hospitals are woefully understaffed and undersupplied, even to the extent of lacking basic equipment and medicine. We deplore the budget decisions that have caused this state of inadequacy."

The late Robert F. Kennedy, who did so much to further the cause of the American Indian, Eskimo, and Aleut, frequently quoted the words of Albert Camus, who wrote, "Perhaps we cannot prevent this from being a world in which children are tortured. But we can reduce the number of tortured children. And if you don't help us, who else in the world can help us do this?"

You and I can help to reduce the number of American children who suffer. We can remold this nation's priorities in terms of people, their rights and their needs. And, if we do not help, who will?

CHAPTER XI

WAGES, PRICES, AND PEOPLE

Alice could not have been more amazed at the way things were done in Wonderland—or the reasons given for doing them—than one not conditioned to accept the reasoning of current economic practice would be today on hearing explanations of official government economic policy.

Ours is the country with the greatest productive capacity and the greatest demand for goods and products, the greatest need for housing and the greatest ability to build houses, the best educated and most skilled work force with the largest demand for jobs and the greatest need for full employment of labor.

Yet, in early 1970, official statements by the government and its economic policy spokesmen before Congressional committees and in other forums actually were going something like this:

"I'm glad to report that plant capacity is more idle this month than last, and it will probably be more idled still.

"I'm pleased to tell you that construction generally is proceeding at a slower pace, and housing starts are down sharply.

"Further, it is a hopeful sign that unemployment has now risen to five per cent, and I believe that we can expect to see it go even higher.

"Gentlemen, all of these things indicate that we are finally turning the corner, getting control of the economy and heading back toward the economic stability which we desire."

While the words are fanciful, the import of this speech is factual.

Lord Keynes, the father of the "New Economics," once said that "There is no harm in being sometimes wrong—especially if one is promptly found out." It is high time that present economic policies were found out.

Inflation had become a burdensome problem during the last part of the Administration of President Lyndon B. Johnson. The Congress and the country had desired to believe that we could have both guns and butter. The expected duration of the Vietnam war and its costs were greatly underestimated. The recommendation for additional taxes to pay for the war was too slow in being sent to the Congress, and the Congress thereafter was too slow in acting upon it.

President Nixon then made control of inflation one of the three principal issues of his 1968 Presidential campaign. Many hoped, as was promised, that the policies of his administration would bring economic stability.

Instead, as President Nixon's term in office passed the halfway mark, inflation had increased and was continuing at an intolerable rate. Unemployment had risen from 3.3 per cent to 6 per cent, and interest rates had risen to their highest level since the Civil War—all at the same time.

America's housing industry became more depressed and less able to meet the housing crisis, and depressed profits in most industries—with the exception of the big banks—increased failures of small businesses and an increasing lack of confidence in the economy generally and in the economic policies of the government were the acute symptoms of serious economic ills.

For a good while, various official spokesmen regularly assured the country that the "game plan" of the Administration was working and that the effort to keep the economy on the right track was near "schedule." Events proved these statements to be too optimistic. And optimistic statements proved to be no substitute for effective policy.

President Nixon, because of his campaign pledge to the contrary or his misreading of the economic situation, or both, failed at the beginning of his term to take up with sufficient speed the offer of President Johnson for a joint and bipartisan request to continue the temporary 10 per cent surtax.

Another initial mistake made by the Nixon Administration was its announcement against any voluntary guideposts or guidelines on wages and prices, even in the basic industries. Such an income plan based upon voluntary restraint, though by no means perfect, could have, coupled with the proper monetary and fiscal action, served as a very useful component of effective policy.

The announcement of the "hands-off" attitude which the Nixon Administration intended to follow, on the other hand, proved a direct encouragement to inflationary increases. The country saw prices in such basic industries as steel and copper go up several times during 1969 and 1970. Basic price increases such as these had great effect on the rest of the economy.

Further, the Nixon Administration mistakenly continued to recommend unnecessarily high appropriations for nonessential military and other purposes. It called for the funding of the ABM and the SST. There was not rapid enough movement to disengage from the Indochina war. The Administration was not willing to join in Congressional efforts to reduce the numbers of U.S. troops stationed in Europe. Consequently, contrary to predictions, the 1970 budget and the 1971 budget request became deficit budgets.

Actually, there never was a real surplus in the 1971 budget recommended by President Nixon. Despite the fact that it gained cash on the credit side of the ledger by recommending a one-shot sale of strategic reserve material, the budget erroneously overestimated revenue—particularly corporate revenue—and made unjustified assumptions based upon the unrealistic hope that personnel pay raises could be deferred and postal rate increases could be swiftly enacted as recommended.

The fiscal situation being what it was, the Federal Reserve Board steadfastly pursued its high-interest-rate, tight-money policy for too long. This policy, concurred in by the Administration, inevitably produced all of the unfair distortions and inequitable effects too much reliance on monetary policy always creates in our economy. The burden is unfairly distributed, and credit does not get where it is needed most or where the proper social goals require it to go.

Thus, as a result of these government policies, while there were huge and growing backlogs in housing needs, home construction was drastically slowed.

While there was tremendous demand for goods and products, idle plant capacity was purposely forced upward.

While hundreds of thousands were already looking for work, the unemployment rate was deliberately pushed higher. Overtime—the margin that a great many people live on—was eliminated or reduced for millions of workers.

It is a wretched and heartless policy that makes men go jobless in order to slow down the economy. It is particularly indefensible to increase the numbers of the jobless without providing for a decent income-maintenance system and a manpower program which assures a job for all those who are willing and able to work.

We should not fool ourselves into believing that we can get our nation's economy back on a fully acceptable basis until we have liquidated our involvement in the war in Indochina. But neither can we continue to rely entirely upon traditional fiscal and monetary policy.

I believe that we should create, as legislation I have proposed would do, a National Economic Equity Board, appointed by the President, with the power to set voluntary guidelines on prices, wages, fees, services, and other forms of income. This legislation would institutionalize what has come to be called "jawboning" and would use public opinion to help keep increases within some reasonable and justifiable limits.

The legislation would establish a larger Advisory Commission for the Board, made up of representatives from labor, management, government, the consumer, the financial community, and other segments of our society, to monitor the economy and from time to time make recommendations to the Congress and the President for additional steps necessary to improve economic stability and to establish means by which all these groups can better work together.

While voluntary guidelines alone will not provide

all the answers needed, it is a well-documented fact that the increase in prices in certain key industries was considerably less when guidelines were in effect during the Johnson Administration than the 6-per-cent rate of such price increases which occurred after the adoption of the hands-off policy of the Nixon Administration.

The National Economic Equity Board would, after study and hearings, prepare and publish criteria which would enable all concerned, including the general public, to judge whether proposed increases in prices, wages, fees, services, and other forms of income would or would not be in the public interest.

In the event any action taken by management, labor, any professional groups, or others, with regard to prices, wages, or other forms of income was unjustified and contrary to the people's interest, the Board would have the responsibility of fully informing the public about such a decision and its effect. Any particular economic decision made or about to be made could be the subject of hearings by the Board. The mere prospect of such public hearings could make a difference in some decisions.

The Board would also have the responsibility of examining key decisions of the federal government that might have significant economic impact.

Without a national incomes policy for some restraint on increases in wages, prices, and other income, actions are taken which have immediate and dramatic effect upon the lives of millions of people who have had no way of participating in the making of such decisions. If the President of the United States, elected by the people, refuses to intervene in any manner in these decisions, the people are totally unrepresented in such decisions, which nevertheless directly affect their lives.

President Nixon's long-heralded economic message of mid-1970 did little to indicate a willingness on his part to assume his rightful responsibility in the field of economic policy. His announcement of a new committee to study how productivity might be increased was so vague as to be meaningless, and his announcement that henceforth the Council of Economic Advisors would issue "inflation alerts" on wage and price decisions represented an unwise step toward mixing operational duties with the Council's other considerable responsibilities and, since such alerts were to be advisory only and were to be issued, if at all, after the wage and price decisions to which they related had already been made, they were assured in advance of virtually no impact.

The National Economic Equity Board, under the legislation I have proposed, would have the important additional power to trigger the credit-rationing system which has already been enacted into law by the Congress and which President Nixon has refused to use. The Federal Reserve Board and President Nixon have caused interest rates on borrowed money to be raised too high and the supply of money to be tightened too much in order to slow down the economy. Such high interest rates across the board do not solve the problem of inflation. The proper social goals are not served. Those who can pay the increased interest still get credit. A few people make a great deal of extra money, all to the great detriment of the majority of people.

Legislation enacted by the Congress in 1969 would provide for voluntary credit rationing—mandatory if necessary—upon the decision of the President. Similar powers were granted to the President during the Korean War. The legislation I have proposed would allow such credit rationing to be instituted by action of the National Economic Equity Board, so that presently outrageous interest rates would come down and money would be allowed to go where it is needed most.

Finally, the National Economic Equity Board would have the power, if it found it necessary, to institute price and wage freezes for up to six months, especially in times of economic crisis, to halt an inflationary spiral. As a safeguard, Congress could by concurrent resolution veto or terminate any such freeze instituted by the Board.

Among professional economists there is almost uniform antipathy toward wage and price controls, but I believe that, as Professor John Kenneth Galbraith has said, more and more economists will come to accept some aspect of this remedy, because there is no suitable alternative.

I hope we have learned some important economic lessons in recent years—particularly that our resources are not unlimited and that if effective economic action is delayed, increasingly difficult economic problems result.

We know a great deal more about how to get our economy moving than we do about how to bring back stability after the economy has gotten out of hand.

When the economy gets out of hand, as it did in 1969 and 1970, the economic indicators become increasingly confused and conflicting, and each new report is more disturbing—and presents no more clear a signal—than the last. In such a time, as columnist Tom Braden said, the government seems to be fighting inflation in the morning and recession in the afternoon. Especially in such circumstances, the economy cannot be allowed to drift. Inaction is action—but a worse kind of action because its results are less controllable.

In such a period of serious instability, the basic flaw in modern economic theory is most clearly revealed: the country must, it is said, suffer either from higher inflation or higher unemployment—and sometimes both. Viewing what Professor Melville J. Ulmer of the University of Maryland has called "the Social Menu Curve," one sees that over the years our economic policies have caused the American economy to move up or down on a curved line, one direction being toward higher prices, the other toward higher unemployment. "All the New Economics does is to move us from one point on the curve to the other," Professor Ulmer wrote in the *New Republic*. "And so we have moved, back and forth, under Truman, Eisenhower, Kennedy and Johnson, sometimes fleeing 'excessive' unemployment, sometimes fleeing 'excessive' inflation."

Economists and the rest of us used to think that business cycles were inevitable and that booms and busts inexorably followed each other in predictable succession. In order to understand the economy, it was believed, one needed primarily to know what point in the cycle the economy had attained. Government agencies put out regular "business cycle" reports.

Now, the idea that recessions or depressions will always follow periods of high prosperity, bad times follow good and good times follow bad is as old-fashioned as the idea that man must not attempt to navigate the heavens and beyond because God did not so ordain.

The "trade-off" between unemployment and inflation is an equally outdated and unnecessary notion, and the practice of raising interest rates across the board, with no differentiation between industries or regions or types of credit need, is as unfair as causing the rain to fall upon the just and the unjust.

If we persist in holding rigidly to present economic practice and theory rather than considering them for what they are, progressive steps along the path toward ultimately more workable and more acceptable theory and practice, the great majority of the people will from time to time continue to suffer cures which are in many ways as bad as the disease.

CHAPTER XII

INCOME
FOR THE PEOPLE

★ ★ ★ ★

★ ★ ★

In his era of economic crisis, President Franklin D. Roosevelt declared "These unhappy times call for the building of plans . . . that build from the bottom up and not from the top down, that put their faith once more in the forgotten man at the bottom of the economic pyramid." Today, more and more, the middle-income taxpayer and the wage-earner feel that they have become the modern forgotten men.

It is they who rightly resent that their sons are more likely to be drafted than the sons of the affluent, and that is why student and other automatic deferments must be eliminated and the lottery system perfected.

It is they who bear a disproportionate share of the

costs, social and otherwise, of racial integration, and that is why special federal subsidies should be given, for example, to school districts in which integration is taking place. They should not be just as good as, but superior to, other schools. There should be special rewards for carrying the extra social burdens of possible racial friction and heightened fears.

A man and his family should not be penalized for being slightly above the poverty line, making them ineligible for special medical attention, for day care center services or extra education and training opportunities. Such programs as these—as, for example, through universal health insurance—must be expanded so as to take account of the sometimes nearly overwhelming needs of the middle-income taxpayer and wage-earner, who is justified in his vehement complaint that government is unfair to the man in the middle, while catering to those above and below him on the economic scale.

In 1969, the anger of the man in the middle at having to pay more than his just share of taxes to support needed social programs, while he knew a great many wealthy people were less fully taxed, reached the white-hot, critical-mass stage. The explosion rocked the halls of Congress. Tax reforms were enacted, rates were changed and the personal exemption was increased to provide more basic fairness in the income tax system which had grown increasingly regressive over the years. Unfortunately, initial legislative progress toward equitable taxation cooled off public indignation and the tax reform drive was halted far short of its goal.

From 1929 to 1949 the percentage of the country's total wealth owned by the top 1 per cent of the people declined from 36.3 per cent to 20.8 per cent. Thereafter, the trend was reversed, so that by 1961 1 per cent of the people owned 28 per cent of the nation's wealth. In 1967, the top 5 per cent of the people in America received more than 40 per cent of the national income.

When I grew up during the depression of the 1930s, my father worked as a teamster or "mule skinner," at painting water towers, or at whatever odd jobs he could find, and the New Deal programs rightly concentrated on the basics: a job, a place to live, something to wear, and enough to eat. Since then most Americans have moved into the middle class, but there is still an endemic maldistribution of wealth and income.

That is why Congress should pass more stringent tax reforms, such as a tax on capital gains at death and a minimum income tax which would take a deeper bite into the huge incomes that now can use one or more legal tax shelters to accomplish accumulated income through tax avoidance.

It must also be recognized that a wage-earner today pays Social Security taxes under a regressive, ungraduated system with an upward limit on the amount of salary taxed. Unless greatly needed increased Social Security benefits are financed from general revenue, as they should be, rather than from increased Social Security rates, the wage-earner may rebel against any more "deducts" from his check.

Wider coverage and higher minimum wage levels are required. That agriculture workers are not protected by unemployment compensation or by laws which give them the right to organize and bargain collectively can be tolerated no longer.

The establishment of a powerful and permanent separate consumer protection agency in the federal government and vigorous prosecution of price-fixing and unlawful monopolies are also important tools which must be fully used to prevent such improper accumulation of wealth and to assure to the average citizen the full economic power to which he is entitled.

The maldistribution of people—the increasing concentration of population in our country in a few large cities—is as much a problem for America as maldistribution of wealth and income, and the two often go hand in hand. Concentration in population centers tends to render people more anonymous, less powerful, and less important as individuals—particularly if they are poor and assimilation is less likely. Density of population tends to aggravate problems of pollution, transportation, and crime. Yet, government policy, consciously or unconsciously, has had the effect over the years of encouraging migration from rural areas and small towns into the cities. This rural-to-urban population shift in our country continues, but gross figures concerning migration of population or unemployment do not tell the whole story.

It is precisely those groups—Appalachian whites, American Indians, Spanish-speaking Americans, and rural Negroes from the South—which have the most ethnic or linguistic or cultural visibility and special inhibitions against assimilation that are most likely to continue to migrate to the cities.

These groups, which make up less than 20 per cent of the rural population in the United States, nevertheless contribute about 50 per cent of the net migration from the rural areas to the urban centers. These groups average more than four children for each married woman between the ages of thirty-five and forty-four, a level of childbearing sufficient for these groups to double in population in one generation.

These groups with high fertility also have an unusually low median age, which also contributes to their high birth rate: 17.6 years was the median age for rural Indians in 1960, the average for rural Negroes and Mexican Americans was about 19.1, and for Southern Appalachian whites, it was twenty-two years—compared with the median age of the rest of the country's rural population of about thirty, with some areas going as high as thirty-five to forty years.

If we are going to make national policy on the basis of people's basic needs and more fully utilize our human resources, we must bring people and jobs more closely together.

Why do people move? Some move, as someone has said, "because they have already seen all the girls in town"; they move to escape dullness and to open up new vistas in their lives. But, mostly, people move in the hope of finding better opportunities. In the case of moves to the central cities, that hope is not always realized.

There are strong arguments for the development of new towns and special programs for economic development and expansion of private jobs in areas of concentrated unemployment, rural and urban. Regional economic development commissions can serve as halfway houses between the states and the federal government and can give better coordination and focus to federal, state, and local efforts to improve economic opportunity in underdeveloped areas of the country.

Other, more fundamental remedies can get at the basic reasons for outmigration, while assuring maximum individual choice and self-determination, treating people the same wherever they live and guarding against side effects which cannot always be foreseen.

These remedies are suggested by the characteristics of the areas from which the greatest migrations originate. Such an area is generally one in which the residents have a low level of skills and education. Typically agriculture and mining, which once predominated, have now declined. Racial barriers are frequently high, and average family income and total wealth are generally severely low.

All these characteristics feed on each other, and each makes the others worse. Schools are poor because there is insufficient wealth and income to support them. The skills and education of the people are poor because of bad schools or racial barriers or because of the background of the children, which frequently includes bad health and poor nutrition—or some combination of these. The income of the people is low because of the low level of their skills and education and because the lack of a sufficiently trained and educated work force is a serious obstacle to the development of industrial and other private jobs in the area.

Increased national investment in education and training and more determined efforts to guarantee full equality of opportunity are fundamentally indicated remedies—for maldistribution of people as well as for maldistribution of wealth and income.

Most importantly, people need income. It is sometimes difficult for people who have not been poor to imagine what it is like. Poverty means lack of income.

In 1968, the U.S. Civil Rights Commission undertook a special study of a sixteen-county area in Alabama to determine conditions there and to assess the effectiveness of government programs. Eugene Patterson, Vice-Chairman of the Commission, described the life of one welfare recipient, Patty Mae Haynes, and her six children, who live on a welfare payment of $113 per month in Mason County, Alabama:

The sagging two-room shack has no glass windows, simply some shutter holes in the rotten plank walls. Large cracks between the planks admit the rain when the wind is blowing. Rain cascades straight down the roof even when there is no wind. A bony dog sleeps under the dilapidated porch. Inside the house two sagging beds sleep the family of seven. The husband disappeared two years ago. The six children have been tested at the nearby school and found to be suffering from various degrees of retardation.

Mrs. Haynes cooks whatever food she can get from welfare on a small stove in the bedroom. There is no toilet, even outdoors. The water supply comes from a puddle far down in the woods, where a small spring drips out of a rock ledge.

The oldest of the children—the oldest of whom was thirteen—ate pieces of chicken from a central plate, and threw the bones to the dog through holes in the porch. Then the small ones stuck their heads in the water bucket and drank from it.

The kerosene lamp supplies light when Mrs. Haynes can afford kerosene. The lamp was empty. It was hard to imagine bedtime in such a house.

As a part of the same study, doctors examined 800 children in Lawrence County, Alabama, 90 per cent of whom had never seen a doctor before. Four out of five of these children were found to be suffering from anemia—almost entirely caused by malnutrition—so severe as to have merited treatment in a doctor's office. Only twenty of the children had hemoglobin counts approaching the median hemoglobin count of most Americans. The rest had only about two-thirds of the amount of red blood which the rest of us have, and for some the figure was one-third. The life expectancy of these children was estimated to be about ten years shorter than that for other Americans, and it was found to be no wonder that they fell asleep in the schoolroom and were generally apathetic and fatigued.

"We heard from a bright, young girl who is a student in this high school, and she said she wanted to become a registered nurse," William L. Taylor, then staff director of the U.S. Civil Rights Commission, reported concerning the typically poor schools found throughout the area studied. "She was ninth in her class of 114, but she was not accepted for admission because her achievement test scores in science, math and verbal ability were far below the accepted minimum standards. She felt that her school had failed her, and obviously, it has."

"The graduates of the Butler County high school, and all the graduates of schools in rural Alabama, are the students who get a Greyhound bus ticket as a graduation present," Mr. Taylor stated further. "They come to the cities, where they are several years behind their competitors, with nothing to sell but their muscle and will to work." Largely the same could be said of many young people from poor-white areas, Indian reservations, and poverty areas everywhere.

Any society which calls itself civilized and tolerates unemployment for those who want to work is not living up to what it calls itself. Plenty of work needs to be done. There is a personnel crisis in health, in education, in law enforcement, in rebuilding the cities, and in other fields. Public employment in these areas should be greatly expanded, and that employment should include training and opportunity for the unskilled and poorly educated to move up to career status. Private employers should be compensated specially, either through tax incentives or direct subsidies, for on-the-job training risks inherent in hiring people with low-level skills or education or inadequate work experience and habits, thus matching up real jobs which actually exist with people who need them.

A job is the best way for a person to get income; it is the most socially acceptable, and it is what people want most. Every person who is willing and able to work in our society should have a job. For those who cannot work, and for those who, working, still cannot earn enough for a decent living, there must be an adequate income-maintenance system in this country.

Jobs and income produce greater local taxes for better schools and services, improved health and diets for higher achievement, greater purchasing power and better markets for business and industry, and the skills and education to sustain them locally.

Jobs and income allow people maximum choice, greater power over their own lives. They can decide whether to live on an Indian reservation or in city suburbs, in a small town or in the central city.

Legislation I have introduced in the Senate to establish a ·national income-maintenance system, the National Basic Income and Incentive Act, is a partial GI bill of rights for every American child. And we Americans should all know from that one example what great dividends are realized by us all, what economic growth, what human enrichment is unleashed by investment in human beings.

We learned from the GI bill after World War II that those funds invested in human development were paid back into the federal Treasury many times over in increased taxes received as a result of increased income made possible by the program. Indeed, great economic dividends for all classes always result from upgrading the standard of living of those in the lower economic levels. But, more important, this bill would result in a great moral dividend; it would allow us all to feel we are living more closely in line with the ideals we profess. We would more nearly be entitled to say that we believe in the dignity and value and worth of every human life.

The bill would achieve these purposes by establishing over a three-year phase-in period a new, fully federal program for undergirding other sources of income for all Americans. The officially determined "poverty level" would become the effective floor below which the income of no American family or individual would be permitted to fall. To the extent that income from jobs, wages, farming and other enterprise, Social Security, and other sources failed to meet this minimal standard, the basic income benefit would make up the difference.

To the extent that we could reduce that gap by measures and policies which prevent poverty before it occurs—by higher wages, new and better job op-

portunities, training provisions and allowances, a
strengthened income position for the small farmer, a
fairer share of national income for the retired worker
through Social Security, a better break for children—
to that extent we would limit the task and cost of the
national basic income and incentive program. It is an
undergirding program, not a substitute for these other
needed measures. Its purpose is to strengthen all of
our efforts to allow people a better chance by placing
the protection of a floor beneath the income of every
American individual and family.

It is time for this principle to become reality. The
nation's governors have repeatedly and rightly urged
the federal government to assume the total responsibility for financing public assistance. The Supreme
Court in its landmark decision outlawing as unconsti-
tutional state welfare residence restrictions—*Shapiro*
v. *Thompson*—made such a federal assumption of responsibility virtually inevitable. Every major organization and study commission concerned with welfare
policy has urged such a step in one form or another.
The Heineman Commission made an excellent report,
and the Kerner Commission also called for changing
the welfare system to an income-maintenance system.

We know now that a decent and livable income
will create incentive for people, while the presently
inadequate welfare system has worked to destroy incentive.

The U.S. Office of Economic Opportunity administered an experimental income-maintenance system

in several New Jersey cities which shows this very clearly. One official, speaking of this program recently, said: "The work ethic in this [low-income] population had been badly underestimated. The work ethic applies very strongly to low-income people." This experiment has shown that people do not quit work when they have income supplements; far from it. "Even where the job is unsatisfactory, there is this urge to work," the same official pointed out.

The facts show that if people are allowed a decent income and have a chance to do a little better, they will try harder. Most recipients have not had such a chance under the welfare systems which have existed in most states, systems which have been degrading and dehumanizing and which have tended to destroy incentive and initiative, systems which in most states have worked to drive unemployed fathers from their homes so that their families would be eligible for assistance, systems which have penalized recipients for working.

President Nixon proposed a family assistance program with a floor of $1600 a year for a family of four with two children, a floor which will provide considerably less than half the amount prescribed for all federal agencies as "the poverty level" by President Nixon's own Budget Bureau in a circular it issued. It will provide income substantially below the amount presently paid to more than 80 per cent of those receiving aid under existing federal-state AFDC programs.

Moreover, such a plan will do little or nothing to help the states with their increasingly staggering financial burdens. Under the Administration plan, the states will still have to meet the cost—virtually without additional federal aid—of closing the gap between an unrealistically low federal floor and the actual needs of poor families. Nothing will be done to equalize the crazy-quilt pattern of presently varied AFDC benefits in the states, including the forty states now above that floor.

Why have we passively accepted a caste of poverty-ridden citizens in the midst of the greatest national wealth in the world's history? We did not count money when we decided to undertake the task of landing men on the moon. But we have often appeared to be prepared to cut almost every budget figure which would insure a real future for thirty million of our poorest fellow Americans.

Perhaps our very strength as a nation has fostered this strange blind spot. We rightly regard ourselves as a nation of individualists. We correctly prize individual liberty, freedom, and initiative. We have been a nation of frontiers, offering opportunities and challenges for the individual.

In a growing nation of new and expanding frontiers, it was less difficult for the prosperous to assume that their prosperity resulted from superior virtue and extra effort and that the afflictions and problems of the poor were the product of their own failure of will and character. We have retained regressive and punitive provisions in our welfare laws which tend to add the burden of shame to the sufferings of poverty. Not so long ago, we also oppressed and hid away the mentally ill or retarded because their sufferings aroused a sense of shame, guilt, or fear in those of us who were well. Today we still do too much of the same in regard to those who are poor.

We are basically decent and generous people. But we have never fully understood the power of poverty to corrode a life, to destroy initiative, to extinguish hope. The time is long overdue for us to recognize that poverty is a social affliction which destroys the capacity for the very initiative which is so highly valued in our traditions. The child who is undernourished has no real freedom. The man who cannot find a job sees no beckoning future or frontier; he knows little actual liberty.

As a nation, we have justly prized our independence. But we are only now beginning to grasp the full measure of our individual interdependence.

Water can be polluted hundreds of miles from its source. A rise in the price of steel is immediately felt in all parts of the country, in all sectors of our economy. Our sense of community must now catch up with the facts of modern life. Our national conscience, our sense of values, our bond of humanity—not just our gross national product—must expand and grow. A renewal of national character requires that the reality of opportunity for many must become the reality of opportunity for all.

We have been a throwaway nation. We use disposable plates, disposable bottles, disposable clothes, and the list is getting longer. We must now resolve not to be known for what we throw away, but for what we build and save. And, most of all, we must build and save people.

Our recent progress shows that poverty need not always be with us. In the ten years between 1959 and 1969, the number of people who could be counted as "poor," according to the official measure of the Bureau of the Census, dropped by fourteen million persons— from 39.4 to 25.4 million. But, quite obviously, twenty-five million poor people in a country as rich as ours is still too many. We have made real progress over the years in raising Social Security benefit levels, but not enough; we must do better. We have made progress in raising wage levels and the federal minimum wage, but not enough; we must do better. We have made a good start in upgrading the skills of our work force through manpower development training and similar programs. We have made a commendable beginning in creating new job opportunities in the public and other personnel-shortage fields of community service. But much remains to be done.

The best answer to poverty is prevention. We know how to prevent poverty as surely as we know how to prevent smallpox or polio. Any measures of alleviation, however well conceived, must be seen as transitional, residual or supplementary to those measures that will prevent poverty before it occurs.

The ways to prevent poverty are well known to us all. Allow every baby a chance to be born wanted, raised in good health, educated to full capacity, accepted upon individual merit, welcomed to a range of job choices according to capacity and interest, paid a good wage, insured at adequate levels against the economic hazards of the industrial economy, and assured a comfortable house in a supportive neighborhood and opportunities for cultural enrichment, participation in the decisions affecting his own life, and survival into a respected and secure old age.

In this era, these are not utopian goals. We have made a strong beginning in all of them, but we have not carried our beginnings through to their logical development. For example, the Social Security Act was a landmark measure in social responsibility, but old age is still a major cause of poverty. We need continued upgrading of our Social Security benefit level to eliminate this anomaly for those outside our wage system.

The Fair Labor Standards Act was another such landmark measure. But even for those covered by its present minimum wage provisions, a full-time worker with average family responsibilities may still earn less than the officially designated poverty income level, while there are millions not covered by the law who earn substantially less. Thus, a basic attack on poverty must include higher minimum wages and broader coverage. Moreover, we must assure—as the legislation I have proposed does—that hunger and deprivation of benefits will never be used to force an indi-

vidual to take a job below the federal minimum wage
level or to undercut the standards of fellow workers
by a requirement that he take a job involved in a labor
dispute or one at less than prevailing or minimum
wage rates. The failure of the Nixon proposal to afford
protection against such practices constitutes a most
serious threat to the health of the economy. It may be
well to remember that similar practices under the poor
law brought 27 per cent of the population of England
and Wales onto the relief rolls in the early nineteenth
century and delayed the upgrading of labor standards
required by the Industrial Revolution. The very aim
of reducing dependency, so strongly emphasized in the
President's message, could thus be thwarted by such a
self-defeating policy.

Similarly, while we have increasingly brought the
resources of the federal government to bear on problems of health, education, training, and job creation,
we are far from our goal of assuring good health services to all who need them, equality of educational
opportunity for all our young people, and decent,
open-ended job opportunities for all who are able to
work. We therefore need to enact a universal health
insurance program and to fulfill the national commitment announced and begun in regard to education.
Above all, we need an updated manpower program,
so that a guaranteed job, stated in effect as a national
goal by the Full Employment Act of 1945, becomes
more than rhetoric. We need the fullest utilization of
all our potential and presently wasted manpower.

The National Basic Income and Incentive Act would encourage individual effort by disregarding in the calculation of resources all of the first $75 a month of outside earnings, half of the next $150, and a quarter of the remainder, until the full basic income benefit level is reached.

Mothers of preschool and school-age children, persons over age sixty-five, and disabled persons would be exempt from any requirement to work. But, should they choose to do so, they would be able to retain a portion of their earnings. Beneficiaries would be assured of the right to receive a prompt determination of eligibility—eligibility based on a declaration of resources and family circumstances, not on demeaning and recurring investigations.

This is an important matter. Even on a dollars-and-cents basis, the infringements on privacy and self-respect which the present method of welfare investigations entail, and the wasting thereby of valuable skills which social workers possess, are not warranted. Despite what a lot of people believe, welfare fraud has been discovered in careful spot checks to involve only half of 1 per cent of the total number of persons receiving assistance.

If America puts first things first, if we get our priorities straight, if we put people ahead of SSTs and ABMs and manned Mars landings and a mistaken continuation of the war in Vietnam, we can easily do what needs to be done, what humanity requires.

If Americans make up their minds to it, we can stop

the suffering of millions of women and children, and we can make it possible for millions of Americans to have a chance to be real men and women.

If we make up our minds to it we can achieve our ideals and make sure that every child who stands before the flag and recites "with liberty and justice for all" can fully live the ideal he salutes.

In the process we can bring together people who presently glare at each other across the barricades of disparate income and opportunity by helping them to realize that they seek in common decent income, a decent living, and a decent life.

CHAPTER XIII

THE PEOPLE
AND FOREIGN POLICY

It was the late Senator Arthur Vandenburg who most impressed me with the idea that people ought not to play partisan politics with foreign policy, and I think it was he who said, "Politics should stop at the water's edge."

In any event I believe whoever first issued that pronouncement was right, though I do not agree with its implication that domestic matters, such as health, housing, education, race, crime, and poverty, for example, are somehow less important and are therefore fair objects for whatever partisan advantage or opportunity they may present.

Be that as it may, if one agrees that politics should

stop at the water's edge, there is no reason why one should also agree, as some would seem to advocate today, that morality must also stop at the water's edge. Of those who are willing to admit that governments have a responsibility to operate in the domestic realm on some basis of idealism, many feel quite strongly that similar idealism is not a practical basis for the conduct of foreign policy.

When confronted with requests for justifying past actions of our government involving subversion and overthrow of other governments, former Secretary of State Dean Rusk once responded to the effect that the United States, given the fact that we live in a tough world, often had to operate in what he called the "back alleys of the world" and that, because others did, we frequently had to do things and use methods which were not fully and immediately defensible on moral grounds.

Some very thoughtful people have from time to time questioned whether a government such as ours, which depends upon the consent of the governed, can operate as a world power in the modern world. I believe the answer to that question is "No," if it is assumed that to do so we must engage in activities which we are ashamed to admit even to ourselves. But I believe no such assumption need be made.

Some years ago I was visiting a country in Latin America in which the local Indians, who could not speak the official Spanish language and were outside the money economy and living at the bare subsistence level, represented more than half of the total population, a country in which a great many people were starving and where the economy was growing at the rate of only slightly more than 2 per cent a year, while the population was growing at an annual rate of 3 per cent. I asked the United States Ambassador at the end of an official briefing in our Embassy there if the situation in the country was not a rather classic one in which the Indians could be expected to become increasingly dissatisfied with the country's oligarchical rule.

He looked perplexed, and I asked the question again with more explanation. "No," replied our Ambassador, a career foreign service officer, "the Indians here are not like those in the States; they are disorganized and rather docile. I don't think any trouble can be expected from them."

The very next day I found out otherwise: in one village in the country the local Indians had already, during the preceding week, refused to do the monthly work on the roads which they had, until then, regularly performed without any trouble or dissent since Spanish colonial days. "If the non-Indians do not have to work on the roads, neither do we," they had said when they had gathered in protest at the local municipal building. I learned that there had been a similar recent occurrence in at least one other village in the country. And I also soon learned that Communist-supported guerrillas were operating pretty much at will in the interior departments.

Our Ambassador's words could not have been more mistaken. One would think that Americans, of all people, would most understand that downtrodden people will rise, that people should and will be served, and that there is a limit to what they will suffer if ever they learn that they need not suffer. Yet our tendency and the tendency of our government, abroad, is often to identify alone with the existing government in a country, however dictatorial or corrupt. It is almost as if we believe that governments have some separate life of their own. We should know that, even under dictatorships, power belongs ultimately to the people only, and only they assuredly endure.

"You Americans invented public relations, but you are now the world's worst practitioners of it," former President Frei of Chile once said to me good-naturedly but seriously. "It is not a matter of money," he continued. "Your President Franklin Roosevelt did not spend much money in Latin America, but when he said 'Good Neighbors,' our people felt he meant it."

Throughout Latin America and the world, too many people have the impression that the United States is a militaristic nation and that we are at least as comfortable, if not more so, dealing with military dictators as we are with elected governments. We sometimes rush in with inordinate haste to recognize a government established by military takeover that the widely believed, but false, impression in so many parts of the world that United States policy is dominated by the military and the Central Intelligence Agency is continually being reinforced.

We have spent untold millions of dollars with the armies of Latin American countries, for example. "We must maintain contact with their leading officers so that we will have some friends among them if the army should come to power," it is always said in justification. But, more and more, in Latin America the right word is not *if*, but *when*. During these last years, we seem continually to be witnessing scene after scene such as that of the sad, white-haired figure of the late President Arturo Illia of Argentina being marched down the street and out of office or of the pajama-clad, bitterly protesting President Fernando Belaunde Terry of Peru being placed aboard a Peruvian Airlines jet to be taken into exile.

When border fighting broke out in 1969 between El Salvador and Honduras, each side was shooting at the other with United States guns and ammunition, and one otherwise level-headed citizen of Honduras told me that he actually believed that the United States was somehow behind the whole incident. Ridiculous as this is, it is not an uncommon feeling in Latin America.

Some years ago, I visited both Argentina and Chile at a time when an age-old border dispute between the two had flashed into sporadic fighting. In Buenos Aires I found that the local Communist organization was passing out leaflets charging that the United States supported Chile in the dispute and had fomented and planned the trouble—and nobody in Argentina seemed to be paying much attention to the charge. A few days later, I was in Santiago, Chile, and I found that the

local Communist organization there was passing out
leaflets charging that the United States was supporting
Argentina and had induced that country to attack
Chile—and everybody seemed to believe it.

During my visit in Chile, our Ambassador at that
time, Ralph Dungan, gathered a representative group
of Chilean student leaders in his home for me to talk
with one evening. This charge—that the United States
was backing Argentina and had caused the border
clash for its own devious, unexplained purposes—
came up almost immediately, and it was obvious that
most of the students thought the charge well-founded.

"No es verdad," Ambassador Dungan responded at
once, "it is not true." Then he dealt the argument what
I thought was a fatal blow. I cannot remember the
exact figures now, but he pointed out, accurately, to
the students that United States military aid to Chile
amounted to far more than that given to Argentina.

Some months before, Ambassador Dungan had been
publicly embarrassed when he had truthfully denied
that he knew of any secret United States-sponsored
social science research project in Chile, honestly thinking there was none such, and it had been disclosed
thereafter in the local press that the United States
Army was, indeed, sponsoring in Chile a secret study
of the causes of revolution under the name of Project
Camelot.

"I know you are personally sincere, Mr. Ambassador,
when you give those military aid figures and deny that
the United States is behind the border trouble with

Argentina," the Chilean student responded to what I thought was Ambassador Dungan's devastating answer to him, "but I recall that you did not know about Project Camelot, either."

Such secret social science research in foreign countries was stopped some time ago by strong protests in the Senate, but that is not the point. The point is that we are not yet sufficiently known throughout the world for the ideals we profess.

Our foreign policy has not seemed to be grounded strongly enough in morality to dispel the belief, widely held in some parts of the world, that we are an interventionist, militaristic nation.

New York Governor Nelson Rockefeller's special mission to Latin America, early in President Nixon's term, will be principally remembered in Latin America for his recommendation of the continuation of military assistance and his congenial picture with "Papa Doc" Duvalier in Haiti—the most damaging photograph since Vice-President Humphrey was caught with his arm around Lester Maddox.

Nor do our actions make it clear enough that we are not exclusively dominated by our own business interests. The United States-owned International Petroleum Company in Peru has been an almost never-ending source of trouble between us and that country. On my first visit to Peru I had a long and rather impressive talk with then-President Belaunde, a United States-educated architect and amateur archaeologist whose excellent book *Peru's Own Conquest* blue-

printed so well how that country might meld the best
of the old and the new of its spectacular history. My
visit came just after the United States had cut off
foreign aid to Peru temporarily because of a dispute
involving IPC.

President Belaunde told me that he was under
enormous and increasing pressures from the left to
expropriate the United States company, but that he
did not want to have to do so. It was essential, however, he said, that the United States government help
him work out better and more fair arrangements for
the sharing of profits by IPC. Unfortunately, that was
not done.

In Lima I had found the International Petroleum
Company case to be a strong rallying point for Peruvian nationalism and anti-American feeling. Out in
the country, I had found it often something worse for
the Peruvian people themselves. I had traveled to the
high-Andes city of Cuzco, ancient Incan capital, to
talk with farmers and U.S. Peace Corps and AID personnel and to view their projects. "When will foreign
aid be started up again?" I was asked repeatedly by
our own people. One Peace Corps group told me how
they had helped to form a local irrigation cooperative,
only to be told that the small amount of United States
aid that had been promised to provide for the used
pumps which were needed could not be supplied until
the IPC dispute was settled. "How can we explain it
to these farmers, whom we have encouraged to work

and hope?" they had asked. I did not know the answer. I do not now.

I do know that, when the present military junta assumed power in Peru, one of its first acts was to move to take over the International Petroleum Company, an act which was greeted locally with general popular acclaim. Large United States companies operating abroad have begun to learn that they cannot staff most of their best positions with those who are not citizens of the host country and continue to take most of the profits out of the host country without stirring deeply hostile feelings which, one way or another, will ultimately prove to be bad business for them. Government policy should catch up.

President Nixon made some rather vague but promising statements following the Rockefeller Report on Latin America and the Peterson Report on foreign aid, but thus far performance has not followed promise.

Two-thirds of the world's people are poor and hungry, and they live in countries where a frightening increase in population is far outstripping available resources and lagging economic growth, already insufficient and strained to the utmost. Anyone who feels that in the next twenty years we Americans can continue to sit in our air-conditioned homes, watching color television, getting fat from eating too much, polluting the environment through overconsumption and feeding our cats and dogs more than a great many starving humans have to live on, and still maintain our national security—not to mention our sense of moral uprightness—in such an unstable and anomalous world situation has not thought the matter through. There is no way we can withdraw from the world or escape our responsibilities in regard to the world's people.

President Nixon was right in recognizing our special relationship with the countries of this hemisphere and in promising to work out for them and other less-developed nations special trade concessions. These nations must be able to build their own economies through expanded markets for their products, and the President should deliver on this promise, as he should also steadfastly resist mounting protectionist pressures to abandon, rather than adjust, America's historic free-trade policy, which has been of such great benefit to the American consumer and the American producer alike.

The President has not been strong enough, even in his statements, concerning the continuing obligation of this and other industrialized countries in regard to foreign aid. The rich countries of the world are getting richer, and the poor are getting poorer. Both humanity and our own enlightened, long-term self-interest require that we help to narrow the dangerously widening gap between the have and the have-not nations. Former Canadian Prime Minister Lester Pearson put it well when he said in regard to the recommendation of the World Bank's Commission on International Development, which he headed, that industrialized nations should provide in public loans and grants and private investment for developmental assistance 1 per cent of their gross national products: "Our response to it will show whether we understand the implications of interdependence or whether we prefer to delude ourselves that the poverty and deprivation of the great majority of mankind can be ignored without tragic consequences for all."

The United States is providing far less than 1 per cent of its gross national product in all such types of assistance to less-developed countries, and both the actual amount and the percentage have been decreasing in recent years. Too much of our aid has been in the form of loans instead of grants, creating serious debt-servicing problems for the recipient countries, too much of it has been government-to-government, too much of it has been "tied" to the purchase of goods from our own merchants, too much of it has been taken by other countries—and sometimes sold in this country—as an attempt to buy political support for themselves, and there has been too much use of aid by us, the granting or withholding of it as reward or punishment, to attempt to enforce agreement with our policies.

All this has earned us more resentment than gratitude, which should not have surprised us. For, as Toynbee wrote, "Benefactors are seldom popular, and unless their benefactions are completely disinterested they may not altogether deserve to be." An ancient Chinese proverb put it even more strikingly: "Why do you hate me? I never did anything for you!"

It is crucially important that we change the objectionable features of foreign aid, especially moving toward multilateral assistance in concert with other nations in order to avoid the kind of patronizing and humiliating, interventionist aspects of our past efforts which have robbed them of a great deal of their intended effec'.

But expanded multilateral assistance efforts and organizations cannot ignore the fact that without social, economic, and political reform in many of the less-developed countries, increased development aid will still be, as one observer has put it, "poor people in rich nations giving to rich people in poor nations," and liberalized trade will still be of little immediate or lasting benefit to the poor people who are most entitled to our help.

I fear that President Nixon is taking the social content out of our aid program, and I am particularly troubled by his failure to speak out to differentiate his own ideas from those of the Rockefeller Report, which recommended that we continue unchanged the military assistance program in Latin America and that we treat all nations alike, regardless of their type of government or the nature of their policies.

If United States policy does not make any distinction between those countries which are dictatorial and repressive and those which are freely elected and democratic, in what way will we then differ from the Pharisee, who, with false pride and unwarranted self-righteousness, stood ostentatiously and prayed in public: "Oh, Lord, I thank thee that I am not as other men?"

America's prestige in the world has never been the result of its military might, the strength of its arms. Rather, it is our moral example, the degree to which we live up to our ideal of democratic government and belief in the worth of the individual, which has given us influence with others.

Surely, adherence to our ideals requires that we not treat the same as others a government such as that of the Republic of South Africa, which by law and official policy denies fundamental equality to black people. Either we do or we do not believe, as John Donne did, that each of us is a part of mankind and mankind is a part of each of us.

If we are truly to ground our policy in some basic sense of right and wrong, we should not congenially clasp to the bosom of our friendship and approbation such governments as those presently in power in Brazil or Greece.

In 1964, a military *coup* deposed the elected leftist government of Brazil at an admitted time of economic and other internal troubles. The United States rushed to recognize the new regime within twenty-four hours, and our Ambassador in Brazil said the takeover might be considered "the single most decisive victory for freedom in the mid-twentieth century."

Not long after, while General Humberto de Costello Branco was President, I visited São Paulo, Brazilia, and Rio de Janeiro. I saw the magnificent edifice built to house Brazil's parliamentary body, later dissolved by official decree. I walked the narrow footpaths, bordered by foul open sewers, of the disease-ridden, hopeless *favelas*—slums—of Rio. I talked with frustrated and angry students and others who had already begun to feel the harsh bite of the whip of repression, as the military *junta* launched systematic purges of universities, the student movement, labor unions, the press, and public officials and suspended the political rights of hundreds of its more distinguished political leaders, including three former presidents.

Later, I sat in the office of President Branco, a short, stout pro-football-guard kind of man, who seemed uncomfortable in his unaccustomed civilian suit and whose mild manner contrasted with his great power. "Mr. President," I began, "yours is the first country I have visited in Latin America in which the students are more critical of their own government than they are of ours."

"You Americans always see people in Brazil who are unrepresentative," President Branco replied firmly. "Only a small number of our students, a radical minority, feel that way, and the dissatisfaction you describe is not typical of the student movement or of the great majority of people in this country."

"You must understand," he continued, "that the Communists had most of the student leaders on their payrolls under the former government, and we have stopped their money. That is why they are angry, but it is not a matter of that much importance."

I felt that this man, trained in the military, unfamiliar with politics or statecraft, isolated from the populace and pressured by the other members of the ruling military group, might have been sincere, though quite wrong, in these views. "If I may respectfully say so, sir, I believe the dissatisfaction is broader than that," I had concluded before changing the subject.

While the government of President Branco and those which followed, that of the late Marshal Arthur Costa e Silva and the present President, General Emilio G. Medici, have been able to restore a somewhat more stable economy, they have done so at the expense of the working class (now, even with some modest wage increases, worse off in terms of real purchasing power) and hand-in-hand with unconscionable repression, political imprisonment, and torture as officially sanctioned policy.

A great many world figures, including Pope Paul VI, have been moved to protest vigorously to the Brazilian government the common persecution of priests and nuns and any who oppose the present autocratic rule and the well-documented torture and beatings of political prisoners which have been a part of official national policy. Nevertheless, only lately has our own government taken any public notice of these outrageous practices in Brazil—and then only in the most mild manner. Meanwhile, we have not lessened our support of the Brazilian government. As a matter of fact, according to Richard S. Winslow, Jr., of the United States Agency for International Development, our economic assistance to that country has actually increased from $15.1 million in 1964 to a proposed $187 million for 1970. Increased funds have been used by the Brazilian government to finance programs for "public safety," "criminal investigation," "counterinsurgency," and the training of police.

In Greece, the Papadopoulos regime seized power in April 1967, the first new military dictatorship in Europe since Czechoslovakia was taken over by the Communists. Despite the fact that numerous political prisoners have since been held there without trial and, as reported in *Look* magazine and documented in the report of the European Commission on Human Rights, despite the fact that physical and psychological torture are "officially tolerated," the United States has supported the Papadopoulos government, and pictures of some of our military leaders alongside officials of the Greek government have been published in Athens papers and displayed to the Greek people as evidence of America's friendship for the military dictatorship in power.

Moreover, we have given that government more military assistance since democracy fell there than we did before. Prior to the *coup*, in 1966, we had given them $89.5 million worth of military equipment, a figure which by 1969 had increased to $158.6 million. Military sales by the United States to Greece in 1969 amounted to $33.5 million, compared with only $1.1 million in 1966. We have sent the new rulers of Greece twenty-two jet fighter-interceptors and have loaned them six United States destroyers and two submarines.

We cannot continue so to divorce morality from foreign policy and expect to lessen the cynicism which many abroad express concerning our motives and ideals, nor can we hope thereby to engender here at home the renewed faith in ourselves and our goodness which many of our people so fervently seek.

A more idealistic and enlightened foreign policy will press harder for limitations on strategic weapons, for carrying out the Congressional mandate for expanded trade with the Soviet Union and Eastern Europe, and for beginning to try to learn to live less dangerously with the fact of Castro Cuba and mainland China.

Most immediately, it requires getting out of the mess we have helped to make in Indochina and stopping the killing there.

In April 1970, I spoke in the Senate to advocate an Indochina-wide conference, seeking true neutralization of Laos, Cambodia, and Vietnam, and repeating my call for more rapid and systematic removal of our troops from that whole area of the world. I pointed out then that what happened in Vietnam could not be separated from what happened in Laos and Cambodia, particularly following the military *coup* which deposed Prince Sihanouk, and that the war, if continued, could not be kept from increasingly spilling over into the rest of Indochina." "Already South Vietnamese troops have been invited to help and have been employed in this military effort, and the pressure will undoubtedly mount for the use of American forces as well," I stated at that time in regard to the situation in Cambodia.

"The President apparently is now hearing renewed advocacy of military victory in South Vietnam, under the argument that without the sanctuaries in Laos and Cambodia the North Vietnamese and Viet Cong will be easier to defeat," I warned further. "This argument would only increase the turmoils of war for the unfortunate people of Indochina, and, indeed, put the United States *neck* deep in the Big Muddy.' "

Particularly because of statements in a newsmagazine interview by Secretary of Defense Melvin Laird and assurances to the Congress by Secretary of State William Rogers, few would have supposed that President Nixon would thereafter yield to such tragically mistaken military advice. Nevertheless, he did—and ordered the invasion of Cambodia by U.S. troops.

No possible military result of this decision could have justified the many-faceted crisis it produced: expansion of the war itself; terribly deepened division here at home, made worse by the awful shootings of students at Kent State College in Ohio and at Jackson State College in Mississippi; exacerbation of our domestic economic woes; and the worst constitutional confrontation since the Civil War.

On the morning of the day of the President's 1970 press conference on Cambodia, I watched most attentively an interview of Kansas Republican Robert Dole, the Nixon Administration's staunchest and most devoted Senate defender, on the NBC *Today* show, because I felt that what he had to say would be a preview of what the President could be expected to say that night. Senator Dole began the interview by stating that he had no power to speak for the President, but then said he had on the preceding evening discussed the Cambodian situation with Secretary of Defense Laird and that he fully expected no use of American troops in Cambodia.

I was even more reassured when I learned that my colleague in the Senate, Republican Henry Bellmon of Oklahoma, who was Nixon's preconvention 1968 Presidential campaign manager, had indicated in an April 28 interview in the Tulsa *Tribune* that American troops would not be used in Cambodia. "U.S. Senator Henry Bellmon predicted flatly today that President Nixon will not send American troops into Cambodia," the news story began.

It continued: " 'I'd be very surprised if this country gets involved in a military way in Cambodia,' the Billings Republican declared. 'I do not believe this country will send troops into Cambodia.' "

But, unbelievable as it was, it happened. While it turned out that the Viet Cong and the North Vietnamese apparently knew two or three days in advance that the United States was going to invade Cambodia, the members of the United States Senate learned it for the first time from the President's television address.

Never before in all of the history of the United States had American troops been sent across an international border in an act of war without prior approval of the Congress. Not only had there not been prior approval by the Congress, there had not even been prior notification to the Congress. There had not even been prior notification to *some members* of the Congress—not to the leadership, not to the leaders of the President's own Party in the Congress, and not to his closest friends and supporters in the Congress. Moreover, what at first appeared to have been duplicity or dissembling on the part of the Secretary of State in his prior statements to Congress, assuring them against direct United States involvement in Cambodia, turned out to be a result of apparent lack of knowledge on his part of what the President planned to do—in some ways an even more disturbing fact.

For the first time since 1919, in recognition of the grave constitutional questions this set of circumstances presented, the Senate Foreign Relations Committee formally asked the President to meet privately with them, sitting as a Committee. The President refused, scheduling a wider Congressional meeting instead.

Earlier, during the Senate debate which had culminated in the rejection of the President's nomination of Judge G. Harrold Carswell for membership on the Supreme Court, President Nixon had sent an ill-advised letter to the Senate in which he objected to what he charged was unwarranted interference with his right to "appoint" Supreme Court Justices. It was swiftly and correctly pointed out to him by the Senate leadership that, under the Constitution, the President only has the right to "nominate" to fill Supreme Court and other positions and that he has no power to "appoint" except "by and with the advice and consent of the Senate." During the Cambodian affair, he and others made similarly inaccurate statements in regard to his powers in the field of foreign affairs and as Commander-in-Chief.

When the framers of our Constitution met in Philadelphia, they were determined not to give to the chief executive officer of the new government the kind of untrammeled powers which monarchs such as King George III, against whom they had rebelled, had commonly exercised. Thus, they denied the office of the American Presidency the power to declare war; this power they reserved to the Congress. They denied the President the power to raise and support armies, reposing this power, too, in the Congress. Neither would they allow the President to spend money for foreign, military, or other purposes without prior approval of the Congress.

The Constitution's writers would not even permit the President the sole power to appoint his own ambassadors to foreign countries or his own cabinet members, such as the Secretary of State; they required him to secure the approval of a majority of the Senate before such appointments could be made. Neither was the President allowed to enter into treaties with foreign governments without approval of the Senate, and the founders indicated how important the Senate's responsibility was in regard to treaty-making by requiring not just a majority but a two-thirds majority of the Senate to approve a treaty before it could become law.

These carefully thought-out limitations on the powers of the Chief Executive and these specifically hammered-out divisions of authority between his office and the Congress have tended to be eroded away somewhat in recent years.

Aghast at the President's Cambodian adventure, the Senate in 1970 at last began to move more rapidly in the direction it had already started to go to assume again its rightful powers and responsibilities. How can the people's voice be fully heard and acted upon in our government, as was intended by the Constitution, it was asked, if the President can freely decide to invade another country without even so much as giving notice to the people's representatives in the Congress?

If without notice to, or approval by, the Congress he could order troops into the sanctuaries of Cambodia, why could he not have similarly, on his own decision alone, sent them into northern Thailand? Why not into the sanctuary of North Vietnam, from which supplies and replacements were being sent into the South? Indeed, under the same rationale he used to justify his decision in regard to Cambodia, why could not the President have moved into the ultimate sanctuary from which such a large part of the North Vietnamese and Viet Cong arms and other supplies were being shipped: mainland China itself?

In the face of an intense domestic opposition which had plainly shaken him and his advisers, the President attempted to justify his Cambodian decision by making as much as possible of the enormous amounts of rice, arms, ammunition and other materiel which had been captured in the invasion. But too many remembered, as did I, how many times during the preceding Administration similar announcements of such captures had been made the basis of overly optimistic predictions of a shortening of the war and an important reduction in the ability of the other side to carry on, predictions which had not been proved out by later events.

And even before American troops had been withdrawn from Cambodian territory, press reports indicated that the Lon Nol military government there was having to concede large sections of the country to the Communists and was experiencing considerable difficulty even in keeping roads open to the capital of Phnom Penh.

In landmark decisions in mid-1970, the United States Senate passed the Cooper-Church amendment against a repetition of the Cambodian affair and repealed the Gulf of Tonkin Resolution to prevent its future use by the President as justification for other Vietnams or Cambodias without prior approval of the Congress. There was growing support for the McGovern-Hatfield Amendment to End the War by cutting off funds, except for the full protection of our troops, for other than our complete phased withdrawal from Vietnam.

All these efforts, which I co-sponsored and strongly supported, were welcome signs, not only of the feeling of a majority of the people of the country that we had made a mistake in going into Vietnam in the first place and that we ought to get out of it as soon as we could but also of the firm determination of the Senate to require full consultation with it before, ever again, little by little or all at once, we should get into a similar situation, a firm determination that we should apply the terribly costly lessons we have learned.

By other action, the Senate also showed itself capable of distinguishing Vietnam from the Middle East, where our national interest was involved in the survival of the state of Israel, a democratic government supported by its own people, willing and able to fight its own battles without asking for any of our troops and seeking sales, not gifts, of essential jets and other military equipment to balance the continued build-up on the Arab side of arms supplied by the Soviet Union.

War is, as Clemenceau said, too important to be left to generals. So is foreign policy. And both are too important to be left to those who do not have proper respect for the power of the people or who do not fully recognize that they deal with moral, not alone political, questions.

★ EPILOGUE ★

We can put America back together again.

The people clearly rejected the harsh rhetoric, personal attacks, and unprecedented and divisive campaigning which characterized President Nixon's and Vice-President Agnew's 1970 campaign efforts.

The country in recent times had not seen anything like it. First, Vice-President Agnew was dispatched to all points to mouth rather silly alliterative phrases, such as "nattering nabobs of negativism," and to launch extreme personal attacks against members of the very body he was elected to preside over. He attacked every national Democratic leader of note, as well as one member of his own Party, Senator Charles Goodell of New York, as "radical liberals," soft on crime, lawlessness, dope, and disorder.

It was soon obvious to political observers that the Vice-President's efforts were ineffective. Too many Americans viewed what he was doing as undignified for the nation's second highest officer. There was something about his performance which was embarrassing to people. Political reporters traveling with him wrote that his own audiences often seemed a little uncomfortable and were less than enthusiastic. There was evidence that he served to rally support for those whom he attacked.

It was not surprising then, when, abruptly, the Vice-President was soon pulled back and the decibel level of his rhetoric lowered.

It was somewhat surprising, however, when President Nixon, himself, thereafter announced a hectic national campaign swing of his own. At first it appeared that the President would take the high road, that his would be a positive effort emphasizing the accomplishments of his Administration.

But, before long, it became clear that he had decided to lay the full prestige and influence of the Presidency on the line, risking further division of a country already deeply troubled, for purely partisan gain. He engaged in gross oversimplification. He and his candidates were for law and order and against the rock throwers and obscenity shouters, while the other Party and the other candidates were said to be on the other side.

The people were too smart. They would not believe that any Party or any candidate favored violence and lawlessness. President Nixon overstated his case.

On the night before the election the contrast between a telecast of President Nixon's shouting campaign speech in Arizona and a quiet appeal to reason by Senator Edmund Muskie could not have been greater.

Despite the fact that the numbers were against the Democrats in the Senate, twenty-five incumbent Democrats being up for re-election, and despite the highly unusual no-holds-barred Presidential and Vice-Presidential campaign efforts, Democrats remained in the majority in both Houses of the Congress when it met in January 1971. They increased their seats in the House of Representatives and made impressive gains in the governors' races.

The sad result of the Republican strategy in the 1970 elections was that there was much less serious discussion of the real issues on the minds of most people and the difficult problems which plagued the land.

The rejection of the Nixon-Agnew strategy and the election of men such as Burdick in North Dakota, Gilligan in Ohio, and Stevenson in Illinois plainly demonstrated that a populist coalition can succeed.

There is a populist majority in America which can be put together if we will try.

We must confront the interests in the name of the people. There is no easy, noncontroversial way to fight pollution, for example. Some have made great profit from poisoning our air and water, and they must be made to stop it. The interests must be taken on in the whole broad range of important issues—from non-nutritional bread and breakfast cereals to high interest rates.

We must remove the barriers to the people's will. The underbrush in political parties and government must be cleared away, so that the individual has more room.

"Nobody listens to us, and everybody ridicules us," an Oklahoma wheat farmer told me recently. It might have been a workingman, or a college student, or a black activist. These groups and others all feel that some other group is getting all the attention.

"I don't want to criticize anyone unless they need it," the wheat farmer continued, "but Congress sits up there and listens to everybody in the whole country, and the louder you holler and the more dirt you kick up and the more property you destroy, the better ear you have in Congress."

A great many people in this country are saying the same thing, including groups which see each other as antagonists and each of which think the other is getting all the attention. A Louis Harris poll in December 1968, for example, found that 53 per cent of the Wallace voters and 44 per cent of the black people in the country indicated they believed that "what I think doesn't count very much."

Too many people still feel that one must shout to have his voice heard in America. There are, however, indications that a lot of young people learned in the 1970 elections how to make their influence felt through electoral politics.

But at the same time, a great many other people who have traditionally placed their faith in the political process may have begun to stand aloof from it for a time.

In one city prior to the 1970 elections a steelworkers official told me his union had run an intensive two-week drive to register its members to vote. Only one new voter responded, though it was found that five hundred of the union's seven hundred members were not already registered.

Nonparticipation was too often the hallmark of the 1970 elections. Too many people apparently felt that one politician was not that different from another.

The people must be given cause to believe once again that this is their government. Politicians must confront the system and make it work. Too many have been just going through the motions, just putting their speeches in the record and then going on home for dinner with the wife and children.

We must eliminate the anomalous "notches" in our system which penalize the man in the middle. He will no longer pay an inordinate share of the costs of social progress.

Most of all, people must be given a chance to enlist in a cause which is worth being a part of.

A friend of mine likes to say that "You politicians always shake hands in order to be reassured that you're human." There may be truth in that statement, because there is something about the times which causes many people to feel so very much alone, literally out of touch.

The rising popularity of "T" groups and encounter and sensitivity sessions is partly explained by a special kind of modern loneliness, the plain need of people to have something other than a superficial relationship with fellow members of their species. Forced to turn inward by a hurrying, jostling, uncaring, unseeing, lemminglike herd of other human beings, whom they must conventionally avoid even brushing up against, a great many people find needed warmth and reassurance in the mere act of touching one another, even if only as a fleeting part of some new therapeutic exercise.

In some cities, churches and other thoughtful groups have established greatly used twenty-four-hour crisis telephone systems, so that, by merely dialing the appropriate number, any person can get another person on the other end of the line who will listen to the caller's troubles with understanding attentiveness.

The need to amount to something, to be important to someone, and the desire for community, for belonging, are deep in each of us and will not go away.

"All we were taught was to try to make an honest living, get up before daybreak, and work until after dark, and try to make an honest living," the Oklahoma wheat farmer had stated.

I started to work when I was five, because my family needed the money. I have worked all my life because I had to, and nothing else could have made me feel so useful and worthwhile. In high school, until I could find a better job, I once worked at shining shoes in a barbershop and at sweeping out a dry goods store, mopping and cleaning the rest rooms at the end of each day.

There is nothing which makes one feel such terrible

despair as needing a job and not being able to find one, unless it is only being able to find the kind of job which one does not like, in which there is no satisfaction.

Today, a young girl quits a well-paid, steady job as a stenographer to take a one-shot, low-paid summer job teaching art to children from poverty areas. A young man I know is going to travel for a while to think and reflect before deciding what he wants to do with his life. A young lady with a master's degree in history and working for the organization my wife heads, Americans for Indian Opportunity, says that she is the only one of her friends who likes what she is doing.

But it is not just certain young people who feel out of things and who are looking for meaning and purpose in their lives. It is a dangerous and immoral thing— though all too easy—to pit the "hard hats" against the "kids," or the blacks against the "rednecks," and no man knows the end of that. But those who attempt to do so are also ignorant of the fact that these groups have very nearly the same needs and frustrations, whether or not they, themselves, yet realize it.

I am an admirer of Charles Russell, great cowboy painter, who wrote shortly before his death, "Any man that can make a living doing what he likes is lucky, and I'm that. Any time I cash in now, I win."

If everyone's work, what he does for a living, cannot be satisfying, fully satisfying, then it must at least be the means to an end which is worthwhile, the chance to be a member of a community, to take part in a common enterprise, based upon fundamental ideals.

Apathy, violence, and self-destructive behavior are the fruits of hopelessness.

But I believe that if we will but liberate the power of the people and call them to a fresh and common struggle to serve the deepest needs of man, the people will respond.

I believe that we can be led to believe in ourselves once again. I believe that we can rekindle our hopes once more. I believe that we can be caught up in a new surge of daring.

Now is the time.

ABOUT THE AUTHOR

Fred R. Harris, senior Senator from Oklahoma, was born in Walters, Oklahoma, on November 13, 1930.

He and his wife, LaDonna, an active member of the Comanche Indian tribe, have three children.

A member of Phi Beta Kappa at the University of Oklahoma, he received a BA degree in government and history and a Law degree "with distinction."

After practicing law at Lawton, Oklahoma, and serving for eight years as a member of the Oklahoma State Senate, he was elected to the U.S. Senate in 1964 for a two-year unexpired term and was re-elected to a full six-year term in 1966.

He was a member of the National Advisory Commission on Civil Disorders (the Kerner Commission). During his term as Chairman of the Democratic National Committee, from January 1969 to March 1970, he launched new efforts for Party reform and revitalization.

He serves as a member of the Senate Finance Committee and the Government Operations Committee.

DATE DUE

GAYLORD			PRINTED IN U.S.A.